PCP

Gerald Newman
Eleanor Newman Layfield

—The Drug Library—

Enslow Publishers, Inc.
40 Industrial Road   PO Box 38
Box 398   Aldershot
Berkeley Heights, NJ 07922   Hants GU12 6BP
USA   UK
http://www.enslow.com

Ms. Layfield dedicates this book to Muriel Colby with love and admiration.

Mr. Newman dedicates this book to Henry Edwards for his constant friendship and generosity.

Both Mr. Newman and Ms. Layfield express their affection and gratitude to Aaron Roy and Bevin Marie Newman for their enduring help and support.

Paperback edition published in 2001.
First library edition published in 1997.

Library of Congress Cataloging-in-Publication Data

Newman, Gerald.
    PCP / Gerald Newman & Eleanor Newman Layfield.
      p. cm. — (The drug library)
    Includes bibliographical references and index.
    Summary: Discusses how PCP is made, used, distributed, as well as its physical and psychological effects. Also provides sources of further information and help.
      ISBN 0-7660-1927-6 (pbk)
      ISBN 0-89490-852-9 (library ed.)
      1. Phencyclidine—Juvenile literature. 2. Youth—Drug use— United States—Juvenile literature. 3. Drug abuse—United States— Prevention— Juvenile literature. [1. Phencyclidine. 2. Drug abuse.]
      I. Layfield, Eleanor Newman. II. Title III. Series.
    HV5822.P45N49   1997
    362.29'4—dc21   97-484
                                         CIP
                                         AC

Printed in the United States of America.

10 9 8 7 6 5

To Our Readers:
We have done our best to make sure all Internet addresses in this book were active and appropriate when we went to press. However, the author and the publisher have no control over and assume no liability for the material available on those Internet sites or on other Web sites they may link to. Any comments or suggestions can be sent by e-mail to comments@enslow.com or to the address on the back cover.

Photo Credits: Clay H. Bartl, p. 57; Enslow Publishers, Inc., p. 59; Library of Congress, pp. 16, 45, 92, 95; National Archives, pp. 6, 21, 27, 31, 37, 55, 65, 86; Stephen Klimek/Enslow Publishers, Inc., pp. 77, 83.

Cover Photo: © Index Stock Photography, Inc.

Contents

Introduction

The headline read, "Street Justice: Mugger Gunned Down by Victim." It was just another New York story. But there was a far more chilling story behind the headline, leaving one mother weeping, and the public more aware of the horrible effects of a drug called PCP or angel dust.

According to Tony Rice's mother, he was a nice kid. "I never had any problems with him when he was little," she said. Tony's mom traced the exact time when Tony began to change, however. She claimed it was when the family moved to the Highbridge section of the Bronx, New York. Tony was then thirteen years old.

"When Tony started hanging out with the other teenagers in the area, he began using PCP," she said. Tony was dependent on the drug by the time he was seventeen. It was devastating. "It did something to his brain. He wouldn't eat, wouldn't take his medicine, wouldn't do anything. I'd fix him his dinner at night and he'd dump it in the garbage," his mother recalled.

Soon after Tony enlisted in the Army Reserve, he was discharged because of his unstable mental condition. Tony's mother believed he had been in and out of mental hospitals ever since that time. And now, his destructive use of the drug PCP, sometimes known as angel dust, had caused him to be shot and wounded, and to a possible jail sentence because he allegedly mugged a person who just happened to be an undercover New York police detective.[1]

Mark Wahlberg, the actor, model, and rapper who is better

known as Marky Mark, has a reputation for outrageous behavior. As an example, when he was seventeen, he was arrested for assaulting a Vietnamese man. At the time, he was high on PCP-laced marijuana. While he was awaiting sentencing, he tried to avoid punishment by joining the Marines. He was not able to avoid sentencing, however.[2]

In August 1996, production of a movie called *The Titanic* had to be shut down when fifty members of the production crew were rushed to a hospital suffering from what they thought was food poisoning. Lab tests proved that PCP had been slipped into the midnight seafood dinner, causing the crew to hallucinate and vomit.[3]

An autopsy of the wife of legendary soul singer James Brown revealed that on January 6, 1996, Mrs. Brown died from the combination of "PCP intake and atherosclerotic heart disease" while she was recovering from surgery.[4] She had previously been arrested three times for possession of PCP.[5] In 1988, Brown himself was arrested after a high-speed chase in South Carolina. Chemical analysis of his blood revealed that Brown had been high on PCP. Two of Brown's staff members told police they knew that Brown had used PCP for more than ten years.[6]

These stories are similar to many others in which we can trace an antisocial act directly to the abuse of PCP. It does not matter if you are famous or not, the actions associated with PCP abuse always have consequences.

David Toma, who was an undercover police officer in Newark, New Jersey, and upon whose life the former television series *Barretta* was based, recalled these two observations: The first was while Toma was visiting a mental institution where six teenagers, all of whom were victims of PCP, were in custody.

PCP, which can be made into a liquid form, can also be sprinkled onto leafy substances such as oregano and parsley. Most often, however, it is sprinkled into marijuana to make the marijuana much more potent and dangerous.

They were so uncontrollable that doctors, who really did not know how to handle them, locked them up in padded rooms. They all had to wear plastic helmets that were strapped to their heads to prevent them from banging their heads against the walls.

The second story is even sadder. While walking through a cell block accompanied by another police officer, a young man of college age pleaded with Toma to help him. "I've been here for seven days already and they won't let me call my father. Please, I'll give you the number. Call my father. Tell him I'm in trouble. I need him."

The other police officer then told Toma that the young man's father would not be able to help his son because at a party two months before, this well-behaved, middle-class student smoked a PCP-laced joint. When he returned home, he took his father's gun from a desk drawer and killed his mother, father, and younger sister. The young man still did not know that he had killed his family because he did not remember the incident. For the past two months, he had continued to ask for someone to help him reach his father.[7]

In the chapters that follow you will learn more about PCP. It is a dangerous drug and its use is currently on the upswing among drug abusers. You will learn why the drug companies that first created the synthetic drug phencyclidine (PCP) discontinued its use in humans. You will know exactly what happened to Tony Rice's brain and why James Brown led police on a high-speed chase. You will understand why the six teenagers were confined to padded cells and why one young prisoner did not remember shooting his family. You will also be able to trace the signs of how a young person could be tempted to use drugs. You will have a better understanding of what kinds of outside forces in society contribute to the rise of drug abuse and why it may be a greater problem now than it was at other times.

You will be provided with names of organizations to contact if further information is needed, as well as organizations that can provide help in the event that you or someone you know has a problem with drug abuse. By knowing what you are up against when offered the chance to try any drugs, especially PCP, you are better prepared to make an intelligent choice—not to start.

Questions for Discussion

1. Based on the examples in this chapter, do you think that only a certain type of person can become addicted to PCP? Support your answer.

2. Do you think famous people are more susceptible to the temptation of drugs than others? Support your answer.

3. If one of your friends were acting strangely and you suspected a problem with drugs, what would you do?

1
A Short
History of
Drug Abuse

Consider this headline from *The New York Times*: "Woman Gets 2 to 6 Year Term For Crash That Killed 2 Priests." According to the story, a car was stopped at a red light on March 17, 1994, when another car, driven by Lisa Bongiorno, lurched off the Brooklyn-Queens Expressway onto an exit ramp at Northern Boulevard, scraped along a guardrail, and finally slammed into the car that was stopped at a red light.

The passengers inside the stopped car, two priests, were killed instantly. But what about Lisa? Did her brakes give out? Had she suffered a blackout? Had another car hit her car, causing her car to spin out of control? Nothing like that happened. There was no good reason for this accident except that Lisa had driven her car into Manhattan to purchase two ten-dollar bags of PCP. While driving home on the expressway, Lisa decided to smoke one of the bags of PCP, and the rest was history.[1]

Lisa was thirty years old. According to the behavioral pattern of PCP abusers as described by the National Institutes of Health, Lisa probably had her first exposure to PCP when she was a teenager and continued to be dependent upon it until she lost control and became responsible for the death of two innocent people.

PCP is psychologically addictive. This means that if Lisa did not have PCP available she would not go through physical withdrawal symptoms, but she might feel a mental urgency—not a physical need—to have the drug. PCP is easily available, relatively inexpensive, and can cause unpredictable side effects. Those side effects not only hurt the drug abuser but can often cause great damage to innocent bystanders. According to a Drug Abuse Warning Network (DAWN) report, PCP episodes increased dramatically from 1991 to 1993 (from 3,500 to 6,600) and the trend and the figures have held and increased slightly.[2] This may be an early warning of what may be a new, and dangerous trend in PCP use.

One of the factors that helps the analysts to determine if this trend will continue is the attitude of drug users and society in general about PCP. For instance, if PCP is not considered a danger to a drug user or a threat to the safety of society in general, then its use is more likely to grow. Statistics merely provide numbers, however. You have to know what is behind these numbers to make any sense of them. For instance, you must know a little about the history of drug use and abuse. You should know why people use drugs. You should know how they were first used and what medical and technological advances had to occur to reach the situation we are currently facing. How do we know that the attitudes of society and government make a big difference in the way drugs are used and abused? You may want to know why first-time drug abusers are younger than they ever were. Does the family structure or lack of structure play any part? What kind of relationship does PCP have to other drugs? Does that have a bearing on why PCP is so dangerous?

Why Do People Use Drugs?

Most of us find pleasure in our work, our families, our friends, our hobbies, and many other forms of entertainment without ever using drugs. When you were a baby, it was easy to seek and receive pleasure. Your parents fed, tickled, and cuddled you. When you got older, the world got a little more complicated. Mom and dad did not always meet all of your needs all of the time. There were chores and schoolwork. There was the process of making friends and losing friends. There was less time to play. As you get even older, there may be more school or special training. Then there is a job and perhaps raising a family of your own. Sometimes the pleasure of seeing a good movie, playing basketball, or just daydreaming must be set aside to complete other chores because you just do not have the time to do everything.

When pleasurable experiences seem to be diminishing, some people may seek to prolong whatever pleasure they have by using drugs that may alter what the mind perceives. Drugs, however, only cover up pain. They cannot solve the problems that are causing the pain.

Opium/Opiates

The knowledge of opium goes back several thousand years. A description of how to prepare and grow opium appeared on clay tablets left by the Sumerians. The Sumerians were a civilization that began about 5000 B.C. in what is now Iraq. They were most noted for their development of a system of writing called cuneiform that was inscribed on wet clay tablets. Opium is mentioned forty-two times in one translation of the tablets, along with 115 commonly known drugs produced from natural origins. The Egyptians, Persians, and Greeks knew about opium and used it as a medicine some three thousand years ago.[3]

Stimulants

Almost every culture in the world has a stimulant drug that is so much a part of its culture that its use is rarely questioned.[4] In the South American highlands, natives chewed and still chew coca leaves as a stimulant, as an aid in digestion, and as a kind of vitamin supplement to their diet. In other parts of South America, a bitter herbal tea called "yerba mate" is sipped and acts as a stimulant.

In the Far East, both green tea and ginseng root are used as stimulants. In parts of Africa, a tea from a substance called Quat is used in the same way.[5] Many people today in Western Europe, the United States, and Canada depend on their first cup of coffee to "wake them up." It is the caffeine in coffee that provides that effect. What about tobacco? It was used by Native Americans in ceremonial rites.[6] Tobacco contains nicotine, which is both a sedative and a stimulant.

14

Alcohol

Alexander the Great, the Macedonian king who lived between 356 and 323 B.C., was said to have drunk a large quantity of undiluted wine in an effort to ease the pain of the wounds he suffered during the battles he waged to conquer most of the world known then.[7]

In the Classical Age (450 B.C.), most mind-altering substances were used in naturally occurring forms. In about 415 B.C., Alcibiades, an Athenian politician and military hero, was declared a public enemy when he and a group of friends stole drugs from the Eliusian temple and proceeded to deface statues of Hermes, the god of commerce.

According to experts who study the use of different drugs in different cultures, psychedelics or hallucinogens produce hallucinations, changes in the senses. For instance, some people who have used psychedelics mention that they can see sounds or hear colors.

The experts believe that during early religious ceremonies, psychedelic drugs may have been used to add a sense of wonder or magic. It was also believed that what these worshippers drank to produce this state was a combination of herbs, wine, and ergotamine, a mold that grows on rye grain. During the time of Hippocrates, who was known as the "father of medicine" and lived in Greece from 460 to 377 B.C., patients were given these same vision-inducing potions, and the doctors based their diagnoses on the reactions or hallucinations the patients described.

In the Middle Ages, which lasted from approximately the fifth through the fifteenth centuries, psychedelic substances were not used in religious ceremonies, but they were sometimes eaten

15

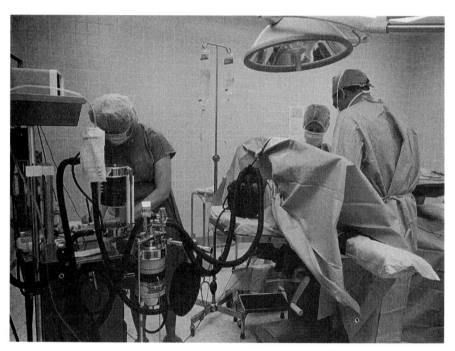

At first, doctors though that PCP was an extremely effective anesthetic for surgery. However, doctors soon learned that after surgery some patients became uncontrollable.

by accident. The person who suffered this fate was thought to be possessed by demons.[8]

After the arrival of Christopher Columbus to the Americas in 1492, other explorers, like Francisco Hernandez in 1576, found substances such as fungi and plants like the peyote cactus whose buds were eaten by the natives, or psilocybin mushrooms. The explorers, in their logs, noted the same mind-altering results when they observed them being used during ritual ceremonies.[9]

Though this synopsis is extremely brief, we can conclude from history that the need or desire to use drugs is as old as civilization itself. It is only when drugs are abused that we have a real problem.

Chemical and Technological Advances

Through chemical processes such as distillation (using heat to separate a mixture into its original parts) and synthesis (combining substances to make an entirely new substance), natural substances have been transformed into drugs of abuse. For instance, alchemists (those who believed it was possible to turn base metal into gold, and looked for ways to prolong human life) during the Middle Ages discovered that distillation of alcohol created an unnatural concentration of it in beverages. In other words, the greater the percentage of alcohol in a beverage, the less needed for a person to become intoxicated, and eventually, addicted to alcohol. This had a great impact on people's abuse of alcohol.

In the nineteenth century, the distillation of morphine from opium and cocaine from coca leaves produced similar results. Originally, chemists were distilling these substances in an effort to

17

relieve their addicting effects.[10] Over time, these substances began to be abused.

In 1853, the invention of the hypodermic needle made it easier to introduce the liquid form of drugs into the body so they could take effect faster. The American Civil War (1861–1865) was the first opportunity for the hypodermic needle to have widespread use. Morphine, the painkiller of choice then, could relieve pain more quickly by needle than if it had been given orally. Of course, the hypodermic needle was invented for positive medical reasons. But this method of introducing a drug into the body also made it easier for the person who used the drug to become addicted. In fact, many soldiers did become addicted. Those who did, were said to be suffering from the "army disease."[11]

It was in Germany in 1892 that heroin was produced from opium for the first time. At first, many in the medical profession hailed it as a miracle drug; in fact, heroin was used to cure morphine addiction. It was said to provide all the benefits of an opiate without the side effects. Unfortunately, no one realized that heroin was the most addictive of all drugs. Heroin was used freely, both alone and in pharmaceutical preparations in Europe and America. During the late nineteenth century, all kinds of medicines containing alcohol, cocaine, and opiates such as morphine and heroin could be purchased inexpensively at pharmacies and in rural grocery stores. At one time, even the soft drink Coca-Cola™, which began production in 1886, contained cocaine. In fact, that is how the name Coca-Cola was derived. The use of cocaine was discontinued in 1903.[12]

Because cocaine and heroin were considered harmless, the average person never questioned using them. During the early

1900s, the typical opiate abuser in America was a teething or colicky baby. Opiates were used to "soothe" them.

New Classes of Drugs

The creation of new, synthetic drugs—drugs that are made completely in laboratories—produced a new class of drugs called sedative-hypnotics. They are commonly known as tranquilizers. These drugs could provide a treatment for insomnia (inability to fall asleep), anxiety, depression, and other unwanted mental states.

The development of barbiturates in the late nineteenth century to ease insomnia led to the creation of phenobarbital. It first appeared in 1912 under the brand name, Luminal™. At the end of the twentieth century we now know of such tranquilizers as Librium™, Valium™, and Xanax™. They were also created to also relieve anxiety and depression.[13]

Synthetic stimulants began to appear in 1887 with the manufacture of amphetamines. In 1917, methamphetamine was synthesized. During World War II (1939–1945), amphetamines were used by combat troops and pilots to help keep them awake. No one, at that time, thought there was anything wrong with this use. In fact, after the war, these stimulants were still being produced, and more applications were found for their use. For instance, amphetamines were used to suppress hunger for people who were on diets. Those people whose jobs required endurance, such as over-the-road long-distance truckers and competitors in sports, used amphetamines. Prescriptions for these drugs were easy to obtain because they were considered safe.

The first psychedelic, or mind-altering, drug was produced in

1856. It was made from the buds of the peyote cactus. Extracts from this plant were originally used in ceremonies and rituals performed by Mexican tribes who migrated to the southwestern United States. This drug was called mescaline, after the Mescalero Apache tribe. By 1919, it was learned that the molecular structure of mescaline was similar to the hormone epinephrine, which was secreted from human adrenal glands and was shown to have a mind-altering affect.

In 1943, Albert Hoffman, a Swiss chemist, synthesized LSD (lysergic acid diethylamide, 24) from the principal ingredient in the ergot fungus—the same fungus that was used at Spring Festivals in Greece during approximately the sixth century B.C.[14]

The effects of drugs in this group began to be studied in the laboratory during the 1940s and 1950s. The focus of these studies was on what they could teach scientists about the nature of mental illness and the substances that might cause such illnesses. Unfortunately, these same drugs were used by some writers and other creative people in the 1960s. They believed that using the drugs would make them even more creative.

In summary, we can come to the following conclusions:

- The evolution of drug abuse stems from a human being's desire for pleasure and his or her desire to avoid pain.

- This desire is historically universal, going back to the earliest recorded times.

- Certain technological and chemical events, such as the invention of the hypodermic needle, and the processes of distillation and synthesis, allowed new drugs to become more potent and easily available to the general public.

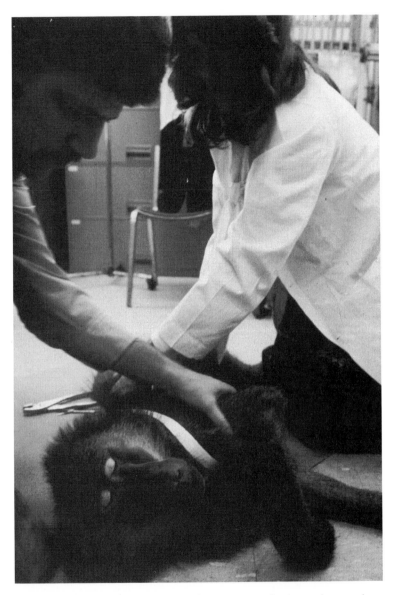

Originally, PCP was manufactured as an anesthetic to be used on animals during surgery or for restraining purposes. When tested on animals such as monkeys, however, scientists discovered that depending on the dosage, PCP had the ability to either sedate or excite the subject.

- The scientific reason to create these drugs was purely for beneficial or medicinal purposes.

- Most drugs fall into four categories:

  the opiates, such as opium, codeine, morphine and heroin, used to treat pain.

  the stimulants, such as amphetamines used to keep people awake.

  the sedatives, such as phenobarbital, to help people to sleep, as well as the tranquilizers to reduce anxiety and depression, such as Valium™ and Librium™.

  the psychedelics, such as LSD, which were used experimentally to determine how mental illness affects a person.

- Society and government allowed such drugs to go unrestricted until it was proven that they could produce harmful effects if they were abused.

What does this have to do with PCP? PCP is a drug that does not fit into any one category of drugs—it fits into all four categories. Depending on the amount of the drug used and the metabolism (the rate at which the drug becomes active in the blood) of the person who uses it, PCP can mimic the effects of heroin, producing a sleep-like stupor or a zombie-like condition. Sometimes, however, PCP can act as a stimulant, such as amphetamine, with a side effect of hyperactivity. Sometimes PCP can also act as a tranquilizer, and cases have been noted in which it can induce a coma. PCP can also work as a powerful psychedelic, like LSD, and the person may react as if he or she is not in a state of reality.

Unfortunately, we have no way of determining how the drug will act, and this is one reason why the drug is so dangerous. There is no predicting how PCP will effect the user. Younger people have higher metabolisms than older people. This means that PCP can be circulated into the body of a young person more quickly. PCP can also be used in combination with other drugs, especially marijuana. Even if you did not knowingly ask for PCP, you might be using it anyway since it is easy to add to other drugs. According to Dawn Barone, a social worker at Day Top Village, a drug rehabilitation center, ". . . there's lots more PCP in drugs that we ever realized."[15] When asked if she thought marijuana should be legalized, she said no. She based her answer on her experience that marijuana was often laced with PCP. She was not sure if there was any way to tell if the marijuana was pure.

Questions for Discussion

1. What parallels can you draw between the abuse of drugs today and the ceremonial use of drugs in ancient cultures?

2. Technology (such as the invention of the hypodermic needle), while it is meant to benefit society, can be misused. Can you think of other examples of the misuse of current technology?

3. Do you think more should be done to stop people from abusing drugs? If so, give some examples of methods that you would use.

2

A Biography of PCP

In 1956 Dr. Victor H. Maddox sent a new compound he had created to Dr. Graham Chen, a chemist who worked at the Parke Davis pharmaceutical company in Detroit, Michigan. Dr. Maddox asked that the new compound, 1-(1-phenyl cyclohexyl) piperidine (initials PCP), or phencyclidine, its shortened name, be tested. After two years of thorough investigation, Dr. Chen discovered that PCP did not fall into any of the usual categories of drugs. Hallucinogenic drugs affect the senses, emotions, and reasoning—often producing visions. Chen also found, however, that PCP acted on the central nervous system to cause both sedation, a quieting effect, and excitation, an uplifting effect. When tested on rats, monkeys, dogs, and cats, the researchers discovered that these animals were either extremely stimulated or extremely calm, depending on the strength of the dose and the animal treated. PCP could also cause catalepsy, a condition that makes the muscles of the body become so rigid that they do not respond to any stimulus. (A stimulus can be anything from a pinch or pinprick to a slap.) The results of the testing appeared to show that PCP, when used by medical professionals, would be an effective anesthetic, both general and local. It would be used on animals requiring surgery or who had to be restrained. Parke-Davis was so pleased with the test results that it commercially marketed PCP as Sernyl™, from the word serenity, peacefulness.[1]

The Discovery of PCP

Because the results of animal testing were so promising, PCP was tested on approximately three thousand human volunteers to see if it could be used as an anesthetic on people. The results of these tests were almost equal to the results of tests performed on animals. One study of sixty-four patients showed that, when used moderately, PCP did not affect the reflexes but did serve as a powerful analgesic or painkiller. In fact, surgeons found that a complete operation—from a simple biopsy to complicated stomach surgery—was possible when PCP was used as an intravenous anesthetic at a dosage rate of 0.25 mg. of phencyclidine to 2.2 pounds of body weight. Moreover, after the surgery, patients had amnesia and did not remember anything of either the preparation or the procedures.[2] In 1959, after being tested on 186 patients, PCP was thought to be the most powerful anesthetic and analgesic available. It did not appear to have a severe effect on the central nervous system, the lungs, or the heart rate and could therefore be safely used, even on the elderly. Patients who were

PCP's effects on a user are unpredictable. Sometimes PCP can act as a powerful psychedelic, and sometimes it can act as a tranquilizer. Other times, it can cause catalepsy, a condition in which muscles will not function.

injected with PCP before surgery had nearly normal heart and pulse rates while the surgery was being performed. Actually, "it had a mild stimulating effect on the heart."[3] Until the discovery of PCP, most anesthetics had a therapeutic ratio of two; that is, twice the amount of the normal dosage could be fatal. PCP had a therapeutic ratio of twenty-six. It took twenty-six times the normal dosage to be fatal. With a ratio that high, it would be nearly impossible for a doctor to give the wrong dosage.[4]

Unfortunately, PCP also had many severe drawbacks. Following surgery, some patients became emotionally excited, often uncontrollable, even to the point where they totally lost all sense of reality, a condition known as psychosis. Some showed schizophrenic reactions for hours after the chemical was injected. (Schizophrenia is one of the nation's most common psychological disturbances, marked by strange behavior, personality swings, hallucinations, slurred speech, and detachment from reality.) Others had nightmares, went into comas, or even died. The same reactions appeared when PCP was used as a painkiller or to treat mental disorders. On January 22, 1965, Parke-Davis petitioned the Food and Drug Administration (FDA) to discontinue all research on PCP. All experimentation was halted, and the FDA declared that PCP was too dangerous for use on humans.

Although PCP was banned for use on humans, it became available to veterinarians in 1967 under the name Sernylan™.[5] The rights to Sernylan were sold by Parke Davis to Bio-Ceutic Laboratories in St. Joseph, Missouri. Bio-Ceutic became the only approved producer of PCP in the country. However, in 1979, the government banned the use of PCP in any form for any reason and thus all legitimate manufacturing of it ceased.

PCP on the Streets

The fact that PCP was no longer legal did not seem to stop those who discovered that the sale of PCP could be profitable. PCP first hit the streets in 1967 in San Francisco as the "Peace Pill." It was given to the musicians and the audience at a rock concert in Golden Gate Park. Not long after that, medical staffs at other rock events treated a number of people who were suffering from what they thought were bad LSD trips. They discovered, however, that these trips were more severe, had stranger side effects, and lasted longer than bad acid trips. They were dealing with a far more dangerous drug. But the general public did not know how dangerous it was. Before long, PCP became readily available in the Haight-Ashbury district of San Francisco, a popular area during the height of the 1960s drug-culture phenomenon. Because it could be made in a kitchen or basement from ingredients that were found easily, PCP became a common street drug, dispensed as a five-milligram tablet.[6] In time, it would be eaten, injected, snorted, or swallowed. When sniffed into the nasal passages, the effects are felt quickly, sometimes as fast as thirty to sixty seconds after usage. The maximum effects are reached soon after that and may go on for up to six hours.

Because of extreme and inconsistent side effects, PCP eventually fell out of favor with the general public. The Los Angeles County University of Southern California Medical Center stated:

One of the scary things about PCP is the wide range of potency in the two commonly-used forms. The people [mostly teenagers and those in their early twenties] involved with this drug, from the makers to the users, don't know how

strong it is and have no way of finding out—except in a
general way by trial [use] and error.[7]

By 1968 PCP was rarely used, according to a report by the Haight-Ashbury Free Medical Clinic.[8] However, it was soon discovered that PCP could be smoked when it was combined with marijuana, and it became a popular drug again. This time its popularity spread across the country. It takes only one to five minutes to feel the effects of PCP-laced marijuana, but the maximum effects are reached within fifteen to thirty minutes of smoking it. In 1970, PCP showed up on the streets of Milwaukee, but it was mislabeled as mescaline. In 1977, PCP caused the death of about one hundred people across the country and sent some four thousand to the hospital. "The coroner's office in Los Angeles found traces of PCP in sixty-six of the bodies it autopsied." About 40 percent of high school students in New York City had tried it.[9]

PCP is usually popular in areas where chemicals are produced—chemicals that are stolen from the factories that make legitimate drugs. The largest centers for PCP trade on the East Coast are in the New York-New Jersey-Philadelphia-Baltimore area, because they are cities near the northern New Jersey petrochemical plants. On the West Coast, PCP is generally traded in Southern California, an area of large pharmaceutical production.[10] In 1979, it was estimated by the National Institute on Drug Abuse that some seven million people in the United States had used PCP. That was three times the number of users of heroin and nearly equal to the number of users of cocaine (9.8 million).[11]

PCP's popularity continued to climb. In 1986, it was the second most popular illegal drug in use, behind marijuana.[12]

Some secret labs are run by employees of chemical companies that are located in important shipping areas of the country.

Washington, D.C., holds the dishonorable record of being the PCP capital of America. There were 4,725 total emergency room cases nationwide that were attributed to PCP in 1986; 1,038 of those were in the Washington vicinity. Out of the ten thousand people arrested in 1987 in the Washington, D.C., area who tested positive for drug use, 58 percent had used PCP. Los Angeles, California, whose population is four times that of Washington, D.C., had only four hundred more PCP cases.[13] In 1988, it was reported that 12,346 people were rushed to emergency rooms across the country because they had had bad experiences with PCP. After a decline in popularity, probably because of the newly discovered interest in crack, a less expensive but more addictive form of cocaine, PCP resurfaced again. In 1993 and 1994, the combined reported number of PCP cases was 12,608—only slightly higher than in 1988 but significant nonetheless.[14] By April 1996, there were 119 arrests for PCP possession in New York City, almost all in the Harlem area. *The New York Times* reported that eight different groups were distributing the drug, which they bought from Los Angeles, making it a coast-to-coast problem again.[15] Getting PCP across the country is, unfortunately, not difficult for those who are really intent on doing it. Once PCP is synthesized or processed, it is poured into soda bottles that are then recapped. It is then not difficult to smuggle the drug right onto airplanes as a common beverage.

Drugs are ranked by the Drug Enforcement Administration, according to their danger and potential for abuse, as listed in the Controlled Substance Act, from Schedule I through V. Schedule I drugs are the most dangerous, while Schedule V drugs are the least dangerous. Heroin and marijuana are classified as Schedule I. PCP, cocaine and some amphetamines, are classified as Schedule II. According to this schedule, while PCP is not as bad as heroin, it is certainly more dangerous than drugs in Schedules III through V, which include anabolic steroids, aspirin with codeine, Talwin™, Valium™, Librium™, and phenobarbital.[16]

When PCP first appeared, it was sold in tablet form. Today PCP can also be injected (although this is rare); sometimes it is combined with cocaine and like cocaine, it can be inhaled in powder form (which is how it got the name "angel dust").[17] Some users have even eaten it mixed with peanut butter or added it to fruit juice. Some have unknowingly been contaminated by having the powder seep in through the pores in their skin, in much the same way that any powder, for instance talc, is absorbed through the skin.[18]

- As a liquid, PCP can be sprinkled on leafy substances like oregano, mint, parsley, tobacco, and most often, marijuana. It sells on the street for anywhere from $150 to $400 per ounce, depending on the distributor and availability.[19] As the price of marijuana climbs, more PCP is added to make it more profitable for the seller. On January 10, 1996, a lead article appeared in the *Detroit News* claiming that the number of youngsters smoking marijuana in Michigan was on the rise. Some parents, who may have smoked pot themselves when they were younger, were not doing much to stop their kids because they thought marijuana was not really harmful. Since the 1960s, scientists have discovered that marijuana is more dangerous than previously suspected. According to a

Drugs are scheduled under federal law according to their effects, medical use, and potential for abuse

DEA Schedule	Abuse	Examples of Drugs Covered	Some of the Effects	Medical Use
I	Highest	Heroin, LSD, hashish, marijuana, methaqualone, designer drugs	Unpredictable effects, severe psycological or physical dependence, or death	No accepted use; some are legal for limited research use only
II	High	morphine, PCP, codeine, cocaine, methadone, Demerol™, benzedrine, dexedrine	May lead to severe psychological or physical dependence	Accepted use with restrictions
III	Medium	Codeine with aspirin or Tylenol™, some amphetamines, anabolic steroids	May lead to moderate or low physical dependence or high psychological dependence	Accepted use
IV	Low	Darvon™, Talwin™, phenobarbital Equanil™, Miltown™, Librium™, diazepam	May lead to limited physical or psychological dependence	Accepted use
V	Lowest	Over-the-counter prescription compounds with codeine, Lomotil™, Robitussin A-C™	May lead to limited physical or psychological dependence	Accepted use

Source: Adapted from DEA, *Drugs of Abuse*, 1989.

representative of the Center for Substance Abuse Prevention, "In 1991, those under 18 accounted for 13 percent of all [hospital] admissions [for marijuana abuse.] Today it is 42 percent. And almost every statistic we look at shows marijuana abuse is highest, and growing fastest, in the under-18 population." In a *Weekly Reader* survey, 17,000 fourth through sixth graders admitted that they or their friends have smoked marijuana.[20] There is a good chance that the marijuana they were smoking may also have been laced with PCP.

Manufacturing PCP

Manufacturing PCP is usually not a planned, organized operation. Drug "laboratories" are set up using the cheapest chemicals and equipment. Police have raided dirty, smelly labs and found moldy bread, rotting food, sewage, garbage, bloody instruments, dead animals, and even human bodies. Many of those making PCP are really amateurs (called "cooks") who usually set up their labs in kitchens, laundry rooms, or basements of hidden shacks. They often board up the windows or paint them black to avoid being detected. Drug agents call these places "clandestine labs," where the small-time cook mixes up batches to be distributed locally. Luckily, these small clandestine labs do not last very long. Informers usually surface to let law enforcement officers know where these labs are hidden.

Manufacturing the drug is also a dangerous procedure. There have been many reports of deadly explosions at homes where PCP was being made. One such incident, in Baltimore,

Maryland, occurred when a group of young people was using ether, an unstable chemical that PCP cooks use to evaporate some of the ingredients. One of the young people had a joint in his mouth while he was "working." The lit joint and the ether fumes in the room caused an explosion. The young people ran out coughing, sneezing, and gagging. Luckily, no one was really hurt. Once the smoke cleared, the youths, who were high on PCP, went back into the house to continue their work.[21] Some cooks, however, have not been so lucky. They have killed themselves by inhaling toxic fumes or having toxic substances absorbed through their skin.[22]

In July 1994 a former Georgia Tech graduate student was sentenced to thirty-seven months in prison for selling PCP. The sentence would have been longer, perhaps ten years, but the drug-pusher cooperated with authorities and named a fellow student, a chemist and research assistant, who actually made the illegal drug in the bio-chemical building of the Atlanta campus. Their product had a two-million-dollar street value. According to a DEA undercover agent who bought eleven ounces of the PCP, "The chemist at our labs said he has never seen PCP so pure. They had to have one of the best laboratories possible, and they obviously did."[23] Lately, however, there are fewer labs being built across the country. In 1978, seventy-nine PCP labs were seized by the DEA. In the 1980s that number dropped to a range of anywhere from three to twenty-one per year. In 1994, the DEA closed nine labs. In 1995 six labs were seized.[24]

PCP is manufactured in large quantities and shipped to all parts of the country. It is then usually sold to one major distributor who in turn sells it to another distributor and from there it goes on to local dealers. Because of this type of large network, it

Because making PCP requires the use of flammable chemicals, accidents often happen. There have been many reports of deadly explosions in secret labs and homes where PCP was being made.

is often hard to get accurate information about where the labs are hidden. Sometimes this information can be found out from the chemical companies that supply the manufacturers. But they often do not want to divulge the source of tax-free black market profits.

In 1985, however, a DEA group supervisor in Los Angeles testified:

> *We took down eight PCP labs in an investigation involving three chemical companies. The companies were under one head and they supplied . . . chemicals [for making PCP] to these labs. It was 90% of their business. We let the eight labs go because we had a bigger case against the chemical company. The PCP labs individually were putting out between 5 and 50 gallons of PCP a day. Always in liquid form . . . . They produced only PCP. No analogues [variations of PCP that are not actually PCP]. Quality stuff. The labs were lightweights. The heavies are much smarter and know how we operate. They stockpile their chemicals, for instance. Sit on them for a while. The amateurs just buy up what they need and immediately go to work in the lab. The heavies deal with a few select trusted associates and they manufacture in huge quantities. . . .*[25]

PCP is so dangerous that a drug bust can jeopardize the lives of the law enforcement personnel each time they enter a lab. Inhaling the toxic chemicals that make up PCP is one danger; inhaling the PCP that is in the air is another. A third equally dangerous problem is having those chemicals seep right through the skin. Officers have reported suffering from "drunkenness, hyperactiveness, headaches, skin rashes, elevated heart rate, confusion, short-term memory loss, aggressiveness, and hallucinations." Female officers have been known to pass their intake of PCP on to their unborn children. At a California Narcotics Officers' Convention, a narcotics detective offered these warnings:

> *Never underestimate the 'glass of water' in the subject's hand. We've had too many officers hit with hydrochloric acid, burned with methylamine, or had PCP thrown in their face—it won't kill you but I guarantee you'll never be the same. Throwing a light switch, let alone discharging a gun in a strong ether atmosphere will blow the whole works up . . . Wash thoroughly after leaving the site. . . . One officer picked up PCP on the soles of his shoes during a bust. He went home and unknowingly tracked it on the carpet where the baby was crawling around. . . .*[26]

What's in a Name?

Phencyclidine is commonly known as PCP or angel dust. There are many different street names for it, however. For example, in Seattle, the purest form of PCP is called crystal because of its white crystal-like appearance. The next grade is called crystal flakes because it has a different texture and strength. If the drug is cut with corn sugar but is of good quality it is called angel dust. If it is a lower grade drug (yellow, moist, and coarse) it is named rocket fuel. A brown powdered form containing lactose is known as monkey dust.

In Philadelphia the naming system is completely different. Here, if PCP appears on parsley or mint leaves, it is called angel dust. If it appears on marijuana, it is called killer weed. As a powder or crystal, PCP is generally called buzz. This crystalline form

Street names for Phencyclidine

angel dust	mist
angel hair	monkey dust
angel mist	Mr. Lovely
animal tranquilizer	mumm dust
aurora	peace pill
black death	the pits
busy bee	purple
buzz	rocket fuel
cadillac	scuffle
crystal	Selma
cyclone	Shermans or sherms
C.J.	snorts
DOA	soma
dust	street drug
elephant tranquilizer	supercools
embalming fluid	supergrass
hog	superweed
horse tranquilizer	surfer
jet fuel	T
killer weed	TAC
krystal joint or KJ or kay jay	TIC
loveboat or boat	tea
lovely	THC
magic	tranq
mauve	wacky weed
mint weed	whack

is available in a variety of colors. In Philadelphia it is brown, yellow, and white. In Chicago, where it is known as TIC, it is also manufactured in various colors, especially green for St. Patrick's Day. Space base—crack combined with PCP—became very popular in 1986 on the East Coast with inner city kids. The combination of the two drugs created powerful changes in mood and disorientation. But whatever the name, the effects are the same.

Big Business

About five hundred dollars worth of chemicals make one gallon of PCP that can then be sold to a distributor for fifteen thousand dollars. Distributors sell PCP in one-ounce bottles (usually in vanilla or almond extract bottles) for between two hundred seventy-five dollars and three hundred dollars each to street dealers. The liquid is usually pea green or yellow in color and smells like soiled diapers. A dealer can use one bottle to treat enough marijuana or other joints of leafy greens to fill eighty-four four- or five-ounce tins.[27] A pre-dipped joint (which contains saltpeter) is commonly known as a kool and sells for about twenty dollars. (Saltpeter is the common name for potassium nitrate. It is usually used as a fertilizer.) So it is possible for two gallons of liquid PCP to yield some $12 million.

Tom McNichol, *in Rolling Stone*, wrote, "The bang for the buck in three PCP joints is substantial; smoking the first joint will make you forget where you've put the other two."[28] In rock crystal form, PCP looks a lot like cocaine, but is yellowish instead of white. A gram sells for eighty dollars to one hundred thirty-five dollars.[29] On the other hand, a half gram of crack, which really is a small amount, costs about twenty-five dollars.

Analogs

PCP is also marketed in approximately thirty different variations (known as analogs). These are made by making minor changes in the formula so they appear to be new, and some even stronger, drugs. These include TCP, PCE, PCC, PCPY, and PHP. Analogs pose an even greater problem than actual PCP. Because the manufacture of PCP is illegal, it is created by amateurs who are not equipped to handle the chemical properly. Volatile and unstable substances such as ether, benzene, potassium cyanide, and hydrochloric acid are necessary ingredients or catalytic agents. The results can be very dangerous to the user. For example, PCC (the C from the word cyanide) can produce cyanide in the blood. Cyanide is a deadly poison. TCP, which appeared on the streets in 1972, is a much stronger and faster-acting version of PCP. By 1975, it was found up and down the West Coast and in twenty-two states. One analog, ketamine, is still (though rarely) used in medical practice, generally as a primate anesthetic. However, it is dangerous. *The New York Daily News* reported that ketamine has been linked to rapes and robberies in New York, New Jersey, and Connecticut. But it was not the rapists who were using the drug. Quite the contrary. They used ketamine to subdue their female victims who thought they were snorting cocaine.[30]

ABC News in New York interviewed teenagers from South Hampton, Long Island, an affluent community. All of those interviewed had been snorting ketamine (street name "Special K"). One young man noted, "It made you feel like you were in a coma yet you were still moving." His comments referred to the effects of a mild dose, but an overdose can cause cardiac arrest in

Federal Trafficking Penalties

as of January 1, 1996

Drug	Lesser Quantity	First Offense	Second Offense	Greater Quantity	First Offense	Second Offense
Methamphetamine[†]	10–99 gm pure or 100–999 gm mixture	• Not less than 5 years Not more than 40 years.	• Not less than 10 years Not more than life.	100 gm or more pure or 1 kg or more, mixture	• Not less than 10 years. Not more than life.	• Not less than 20 years. Not more than life.
Heroin[†]	100–999 gm mixture			1 kg or more mixture		
Cocaine[†]	500–4,999 gm mixture	• If death or serious injury, not less than 20 years or more than life.	• If death or serious injury, not less than life.	5 kg or more mixture	• If death or serious injury, not less than 20 years or more than life.	• If death or serious injury, not less than life.
Cocaine Base[†]	5–49 gm mixture			50 gm or more mixture		
PCP[†]	10–99 gm pure or 100–999 gm mixture			100 gm or more pure or 1 kg or more mixture		
LSD[†]	1–9 gm mixture	• Fine of not more than $2 million individual, $5 million other than individual.	• Fine of not more than $4 million individual, $10 million other than individual.	10 gm or more mixture	• Fine of not more than $4 million individual, $10 million other than individual.	• Fine of not more than $8 million individual, $20 million other than individual.
Fentanyl[†]	40–3999 gm mixture			400 gm or more mixture		
Fentanyl Analogue[†]	10–99 gm mixture			100 gm or more mixture		

[†]Schedule I or II drugs.

Drug	Quantity	First Offense	Second offense
Schedule I & II (law does not include marijuana, hashish, or hash oil)	Any	• Not more than 20 years. • If death or serious injury, not less than 20 years, not more than life. • Fine $1 million individual, $5 million not individual.	• Not more than 30 years. • If death or serious injury, life. • Fine $2 million individual, $10 million not individual.
Schedule III (Includes anabolic steroids as of 2-27-91)	Any	• Not more than 5 years. • Fine not more than $250,000 individual, $1 million not individual.	• Not more than 10 years. • Fine not more than $500,000 individual, $2 million not individual.
Schedule IV	Any	• Not more than 3 years. • Fine not more than $250,000 individual, $1 million not individual.	• Not more than 6 years. • Fine not more than $500,000 individual, $2 million not individual.
Schedule V	Any	• Not more than 1 year. • Fine not more than $100,000 individual, $250,000 not individual.	• Not more than 2 years. • Fine not more than $200,000 individual, $500,000 not individual.

just forty-five seconds. Those more fortunate may have hallucinogenic flashbacks for months after ingesting the drug. Nonetheless, 80 percent of the teens at Daytop Village, in Huntington, Long Island, where they were undergoing rehabilitation, have admitted using it.[31]

PCP and the Law

What are the penalties for possession, manufacture, and sale of PCP? That depends on who does the arresting. If a trafficker is arrested by a DEA officer, then it is a federal arrest because the DEA is a federal agency. If a trafficker is arrested by local police, then it is a state or city offense. At the moment, the penalty for possession of up to a gram of PCP for personal use is considered a misdemeanor (an offense that the law may treat as minor) in nonfederal cases.[32] As a Schedule II drug, possession of between 10 and 99 grams of pure PCP or 100 to 199 grams of PCP mixed with some other substance is a felony (a serious crime resulting in a more severe punishment than a misdemeanor). Penalties include fines for first offenders that could go as high as $2 million per person and a jail term of between five and forty years. A second offense raises the penalty to a jail term of from ten years to life imprisonment and fines up to $4 million per person. Sale and possession of 100 kilograms or more of pure PCP or 1 kilogram or more of PCP mixed with another substance draws even heavier penalties. A first-time offender can be sentenced to jail for not less than ten years. The accompanying fine can reach as high as $4 million. If it is a second offense, the jail term doubles to not less than twenty years, and the fine shoots up to a maximum of $8 million.[33] There are many law enforcement

If caught, those who illegally manufacture, dispense, distribute, import, export, buy, or sell 100 grams or more of PCP are subject to a minimum prison sentence of ten years.

officers, medical personnel, and counselors who are struggling to make PCP trafficking penalties more severe, primarily because of the violence and uncontrollable behavior aspects of an overdose. If, like heroin and LSD, PCP were classified as a Schedule I drug, because the law does not allow any medical use of PCP, then traffickers would receive a much stricter penalty, even life in prison. On February 15, 1996, two ringleaders of a major drug operation that manufactured and sold PCP were convicted in Los Angeles federal court. They were arrested in 1995 while manufacturing thirty-six gallons of PCP. During the raid, authorities were able to confiscate about $30 million worth of PCP. They are facing life sentences for multiple counts of drug trafficking.

In 1993, the joint task force of the Los Angeles Police Department and the Federal Bureau of Alcohol, Tobacco and Firearms also arrested several mid-level PCP dealers. Three of the dealers received prison terms ranging from twenty-two to forty-five years for various drug and firearms offenses.[34]

The two arrested ringleaders were suppliers to a gang known as the Crips. The dealers who were arrested a few years earlier were also Crips. The Crips, along with the Hell's Angels, the Outlaws, the Pagans, the Bandidos, and the Bloods are some of the many gangs that the DEA has been tracking since the early 1960s because of their involvement in the distribution of PCP. It is thought by law enforcement officials that these gangs have created a network throughout the country to make it easy for them to distribute drugs. As of now, though many members have been arrested, the gangs still exist, and the distribution continues.

Questions for Discussion

1. Do you think that tougher penalties for making or using PCP would curtail its abuse? If not, what would you propose?

2. Suggest possible solutions to the problem of illegal drug labs.

3. Do you think PCP should, like heroin and marijuana, be a Schedule I drug? Why? Why not?

3

How PCP Works

We have discussed how PCP is made, used, and transported but what does it do once it is inside the body?

Stages of PCP Intoxication

Though they are unpredictable, the effects of PCP are generally categorized in four stages:

The early stage. After a dose of one to five milligrams, the average user is moderately stimulated or euphoric, showing no symptoms of being anesthetized. Physical symptoms usually resemble those of alcohol intoxication. Some users may appear drug-free, while others show signs of drooling, flushing, and sweating. Users often have a feeling of numbness, droopy eyelids, stiffness, sensitivity to light and sound, and increased urination.

However, some have been known to show rage, anxiety, rapid changes in mood, and loss of the ability to sleep (amnesia), even on a moderately small dose.[1]

One report told of Sandi (not her real name), and her unhappy life with her boyfriend Tim (not his real name). When the drugs they were taking were not getting them high enough, Tim got them some marijuana and laced it with PCP. According to Sandi:

I was smoking it and all of a sudden everything started flashing and ringing in my ears and I was moving in slow motion.

Soon however, things got stranger.

I was standing there in line [to go on the roller coaster] and everything was flashing black and white, and I was moving in slow motion, holding onto the railings; my legs felt like noodles . . . and in my head, my head's telling me, 'If you go on that roller coaster you're gonna die.' I passed out in line [and Tim] had to carry me back to some bench or something, and like the rest of the evening was like a dream . . . a fog. I didn't even remember it.[2]

A low PCP dose begins to work within a few minutes, reaches its peak in about a half-hour, and wears off after four to six hours.

The second stage. After a dose of more than five milligrams, users often feel uncoordinated and anesthetized, especially in their limbs. Their speech is slurred, and their entire body seems to slow down. Some people report that they feel as though the ground beneath them feels spongy. However, their thoughts seem to speed up, and some say that they have had a type of out-of-body experience in which they seem to watch themselves.[3] Blood pressure rises, and the white blood cell count increases. Vomiting, seizures, and loss of muscle control (*ataxia*) are all common. Some abusers become obscene, even vulgar. Because of PCP's anesthetic quality, some people feel so little pain that burns, cuts, and bruises often are not felt. Users can inflict danger upon themselves without realizing it. Some users feel so powerful that they may set fire to themselves or attack others.[4] "Users in a 'whack attack' . . . think they're supermen, and have superhuman strength. Some PCP users have fallen off cliffs, jumped off buildings, or been hit by cars while walking down the middle of a highway."[5] Others have attempted to fight off stick-wielding policemen, feeling no pain because of the anesthetic quality of the drug.[6] Police find it difficult to handle people on PCP. The use of a club usually subdues most violent people, but those on PCP feel no pain.

PCP and Violence. There are statistics that lead scientists to believe that there is some connection between the intake of PCP and violence. The following cases illustrate this point: A thirty-eight-year-old-man who smoked marijuana regularly bought something called "superweed." When he started smoking it, he became paranoid and hostile. He determined that this new drug was responsible, so he stopped using it. His symptoms did not stop, however. He took more superweed, hoping to relieve the symptoms. He became so hostile that he chopped the head off of his dog and slashed a perfect stranger with a razor. When he was taken to a hospital and tested, the doctors discovered that the marijuana he had smoked was laced with PCP.[7]

A young couple, Rick and Martina, were celebrating their honeymoon at a hotel. A friend had turned them on to angel dust.

Late one evening, Rick took a dose. Shortly afterward, he began seeing things that were not there and became frightened that Martina was going to hurt him. He screamed over and over again, "Stay away from me! Don't touch me!" When Martina could not calm him down, she called the police. When they arrived, Rick attacked them. He kicked in the door of the next room, and the guest in that room shot him in the chest. Even after he lost a great deal of blood, it took six policemen to subdue him.[8]

Two high school students who were best friends ingested PCP. One felt tired and took a nap on the sofa. The other began to hallucinate and thought his friend was a wild animal that was attacking him. He grabbed a kitchen knife and stabbed his sleeping friend twenty-one times. When the effects of PCP wore off, he did not remember killing his friend.[9]

A 1980 article written for the *Journal of Psychedelic Drugs*, vol. 12, entitled "PCP and Violent Crime: The People vs. Peace," by R.K. Seigel, indicated that about half of forty-five people arrested for fighting were using PCP; 40 percent were PCP-provoked attacks on people or property. Another 1980 study found that of 112 boys in a correctional training school, there was evidence of PCP abuse among many of them. In 1981, a study found that of sixty-eight people who had applied for treatment for PCP use, 31 percent stated that they were involved in fighting while on PCP, and 24 percent were responsible for someone being hurt. Another 1981 study reported that of one thousand cases of PCP intoxication, 35 percent were involved in some sort of PCP-induced violence. In 1985, a San Jose, California, police report noted that 22 percent of all murders were PCP related. A 1988 study concluded that "15% of 222 PCP-positive arrestees in Washington, DC were charged with either robbery or assault."

The report also noted that "PCP users were more likely to be arrested . . . than heroin or cocaine users." Many of those who conducted the surveys agree that the reports are nonconclusive, but with numbers as high as those noted, there certainly is reason to be concerned.[10]

Third stage abuse. Intake ranges from ten to twenty milligrams. Users remain conscious, but their voice becomes so slurred that words become difficult to understand. They cannot think logically, and they find it impossible to move. Some users exhibit severe paranoia, and some become psychotic, that is, they withdraw from reality. Some remain in a depressed state that can last from twenty-four hours to several months. During recovery from the third stage, patients live through the symptoms of the first two stages. At a rock concert in San Francisco, six teenagers who had smoked angel dust in the afternoon, popped it in pill form in the evening. All six became very high but fortunately, five quickly recovered. The unfortunate part is that the sixth, a seventeen-year-old, went into a coma. "His breathing was shallow and all his muscles were extremely rigid." After being kept on a respirator for three days, he suffered from temporary memory loss and continued to be confused and depressed for another week. Suicide attempts are also possible. A fifteen-year-old who continued to have frightening hallucinations checked himself into a detoxification clinic. Once the visions had stopped, he was discharged and allowed to return home. A few days later, he threw a light cord over a garage beam and hung himself. In California, a woman was arrested for dangerous driving. After she was booked, she stepped into the shower and drowned herself in a few inches of water.[11]

The fourth stage. An intake of more than twenty milligrams is considered an overdose and produces changes in heart rhythms, blood pressure, and respiration. It can bring on muscle spasms, convulsions, and hallucinations. Moreover, overdosing usually causes a coma that can last for just a few hours or as much as a few days. During the coma, the eyes may still remain open, but the users do not react to stimuli. Once they have emerged from the coma, some abusers experience memory loss, psychiatric problems such as antisocial behavior, personality changes, schizophrenia, anxiety, and depression (much like those in the third stage of PCP use.)[12] Attacks of schizophrenia and paranoia have been known to last for a year or longer. One interesting aspect of PCP hallucination in stage four is the common theme of death, called "meditatio mortis." Abusers have what seems to be an out-of-body experience in which they see themselves dying. Some think they see parts of their bodies, especially their legs, disappear. Others have the frightening feeling of being nearly invisible.

With continued use of PCP, "burning out" is a serious result. Users become spacey, making it impossible to understand them. They are unable to think clearly and unable to remember things. Some remain depressed, moody, confused, anxious, aggressive, and/or violent. Others lose body coordination and suffer permanent speech impairment. Sometimes these symptoms can last as long as a year. Worse, sometimes the symptoms do not ever go away. The users become outcasts because friends become uneasy in their presence, thinking the users are unreliable and no longer fun to be with. Friends feel a mixture of pity and disgust. Abandonment is generally the course taken.

PCP in the Body

Aside from it being unpredictable, one of the reasons PCP is so dangerous is that it is a lipophilic. This means it is stored in body fat and the brain for a long time, affecting the central nervous system, specifically the neurotransmitters.

It is important to know what a neurotransmitter is. It is defined as a chemical messenger that moves an electrical signal from one brain cell, known as a neuron, to another. Scientists now believe that psychoactive drugs, such as PCP, work by copying or disrupting the action of neurotransmitters. [13]

Your brain is composed of twelve billion neurons (nerve cells). One neuron is composed of a nucleus and a body. Growing out of the body is a long strand or thread called an axon. Many other fine threads called dendrites also branch out from the body of the neuron, but the axon is longest. Signals are passed along the axon. At the tip of the axon, signals meet the dendrites of another neuron. But before the signal can pass from the axon of one neuron to the dendrites of another, it has to pass over a small gap, called the synapse, where the axon and dendrites meet. At the end of the axon, tiny bubbles, called vesicles, are released. They contain the neurotransmitter chemical that carries the nerve signal across the synapse to the next neuron at the neurotransmitter reception site.

These chemical transmitters can be of two types; some are called excitatory chemicals, which allow the signal to be carried through. Other transmitters are called inhibitory chemicals. Their function is to prevent a signal from traveling to the next neuron. Neurotransmitters carry the instructions that tell the brain cells to stop or start a series of functions. If a psychoactive

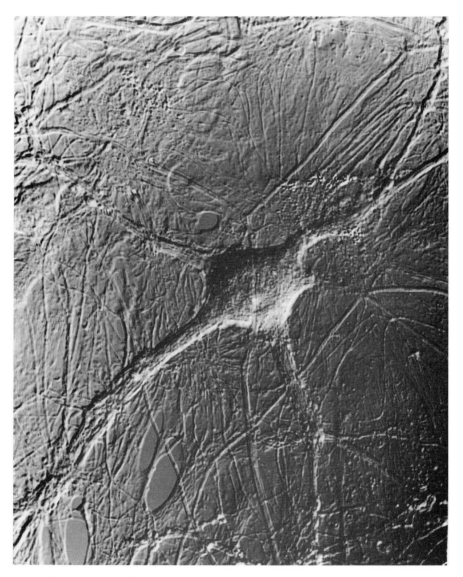

This micrograph shows the details of a neuron, or nerve cell. Communication is made when chemicals called neurotransmitters pass from one neuron to another at specific sites called synapses. These can be found in cell bodies, axons, and dendrites.

drug such as PCP is used, normal transmission of nerve signals is unpredictable. PCP can act to stimulate neurotransmitters, inhibit neurotransmitters, or take the place of a neurotransmitter with its own set of commands that can destroy the path of a nerve signal and may account for some of the more serious symptoms of PCP abuse.

Scientists believe each drug group is associated with certain neurotransmitters and their receptor sites. Receptor sites that respond to PCP have been discovered and may be responsible for releasing chemicals that produce hallucinations and other mind-altering states that make the PCP user appear to be schizophrenic or psychotic.

PCP is slowly released into the bloodstream. PCP that is eliminated into the stomach from the blood passes into the small intestines. Here it is reabsorbed and recirculated in the body. Finally it is metabolized, or processed, in the liver and expelled in the urine and feces. The drug usually remains in the body for about three days, but tests have found it in the urine for as long as eight days following PCP use.[14] The user may believe that the drug is out of his or her body, and then, without any warning, he or she may start having frightening symptoms because the drug is actually still in the body.

Dentists need to be especially wary when using sedation and/or general anesthesia or prescribing painkillers to patients. Some of those patients may be PCP abusers who believe they are clean but are actually still infused with PCP. The results can be seizures, respiration trouble, or a coma. PCP is known to suppress the glottic reflex, commonly known as the natural swallowing process. This can cause vomit to back up into the lungs, resulting in death caused by a clogged air passage.[15]

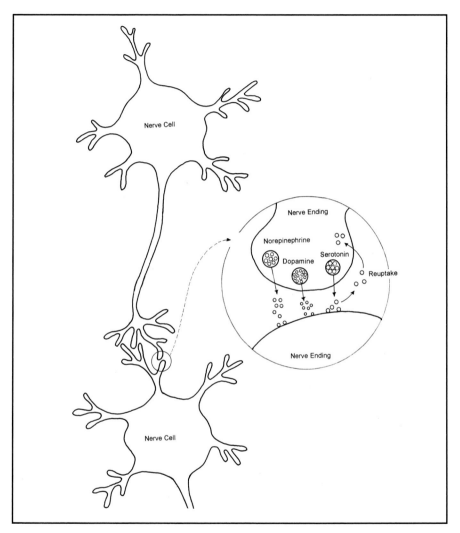

Nerve cells produce neurotransmitters to relay information on to the next nerve cells. Once the neurotransmitters have done their job, they are reabsorbed by the originating nerve cell. PCP increases or decreases the amount of each neurotransmitter, thus producing unusual effects.

Toxic Psychosis

Another consequence of PCP abuse is toxic psychosis. Psychosis is defined as a mental disorder whereby a person's social and intellectual behavior falls apart and he or she withdraws from society. Toxic psychosis means that the cause of the psychosis is a poison or a drug such as PCP.[16] This condition, though often only lasting up to a week, can produce violent, self-destructive—even suicidal—behavior. Generally, however, users show radically opposing symptoms from being in a stupor so complete that they are absolutely rigid, to becoming hyperactive so they are uncontrollable, to displaying acute paranoia. This last condition is a psychosis exhibiting personality swings and feelings of suspicion and distrust and an exaggerated sense of self-importance. Some people believe that their lives are in danger because someone or some organization is out to get them. If they believe that they are being persecuted then there must be a reason, and thus some develop unfounded feelings of superiority. Once the psychosis passes, depression usually follows. This sometimes forces the user to use PCP again in the hope that a good trip will chase the depression away. What generally happens is that the user experiences another psychotic episode. A vicious, dangerous cycle develops with little hope of ending because PCP psychosis is the result of blockage of sensory input to the brain.[17]

In a test, both schizophrenics and healthy volunteers were given PCP. The healthy volunteers exhibited schizophrenic symptoms for a few days. The actual schizophrenics became more hostile for as long as six more weeks. Schizophrenics also exhibit bizarre behavior similar to behavior of those on PCP: Hallucinations, incoherent speech, and a detachment from reality are all

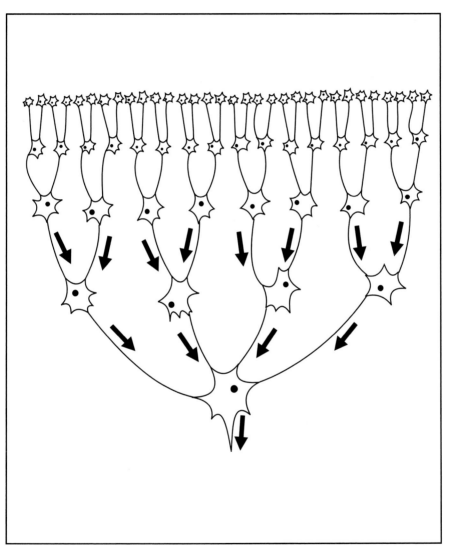

In the nervous system fine branches join and eventually pass a signal through a single nerve fiber.

common. In a study conducted on thirty-five people suffering from PCP psychosis and eleven people suffering from acute schizophrenia, very few differences were found. However, the PCP users were found to be more violent and tended to be in trouble with the law more often.

Use of PCP by those with mental disorders can be devastating. A twenty-six-year-old woman with a history of mental illness but who never before used drugs smoked some angel dust at a party. After just half a joint, she developed hallucinations and became paranoid. After two weeks in the hospital, the symptoms gradually disappeared, but she was left in a depressed state and needed to be treated with antipsychotic drugs.[18] "To be sure, not every user goes into convulsions or gets psychotic and tries to murder someone," Florence Isaacs wrote in *Reader's Digest*:

> *But the risk is always there. A person can take PCP regularly for years with no ill effects and suddenly have a bad trip; others have a pleasurable trip one day and a 'bummer' a week later. In greatest danger are small children, who seldom have much tolerance. Dr. [Regine] Aronow [of the Children's Hospital of Michigan] has treated thirty-eight children under the age of eight—five of them less than a year old. All survived, but some came close to death.*[19]

PCP Tolerance

Continued use of PCP can lead to tolerance, so that more and more PCP is needed in order for the abuser to obtain the same high. For example, if a user smokes angel dust and derives some sort of high from it, before long, in order to achieve that same feeling, the abuser will need to smoke more and more joints. In addition, the effects are cumulative. This means that small regular doses over time have the same impact as one massive dose. If a user cuts down on the amount of PCP intake, his or her tolerance will decrease and sometimes disappear.

If the user resumes taking PCP at the same rate or strength as he or she did before, dangerous effects are likely because his or her brain and body are no longer used to the drug. Since the drug is homemade and unreliable, the user never knows exactly what he or she is getting. There is also a danger of overdose because the user does not know how much PCP is needed to achieve the desired high. There is no antidote to block or stop the effects of PCP. An antidote is a drug used to control the effects of another drug. For example, Narcan™ is usually administered as an antidote to those who are trying to break the addiction to heroin.

Though three-quarters of those using PCP have had at least one negative experience, sometimes called a "bad trip," such as numbness, confusion, memory loss, and delusions, they continue to use the drug because of its powerful effects, its availability, and its inexpensive cost.[20] In a study conducted in the early 1980s on sixty-eight regular PCP users, about thirty-three patients undergoing withdrawal claimed they felt depressed, lazy, extremely tired, hungry, and drug-deprived. The discomfort lasted from a week to a month depending on the speed with which the PCP left the body.[21] In a 1980 study of thirty-five people with PCP psychosis, six were later hospitalized and diagnosed with acute schizophrenia. None used PCP after the original diagnosis.[22]

A nineteen-year-old woman checked into a drug rehabilitation clinic because she was deeply depressed and was considering suicide after a PCP overdose. Her symptoms were only relieved when she snorted the drug. Once she stopped snorting PCP, her

61

depression became even more severe, so she began using the drug again. She decided she would rather continue to snort PCP than suffer bouts of severe depression and suicidal thoughts. So it seems that the psychological pain of withdrawal, combined with symptoms much like the flu (nausea, fever, and chills) often forces PCP users to continue using the drug. Tests on animals confirm this theory. In a study of rhesus monkeys who were injected with PCP, the monkeys experienced obvious withdrawal symptoms such as hyperactivity, vomiting, and diarrhea that lasted up to forty-eight hours. When injected with PCP, the symptoms vanished.[23] In humans, however, there is an emotional factor. PCP can ruin the lives of users. Some users, however, perceive that PCP's effects are still better than the depressing low they have without PCP.[24] This is a common emotional dilemma among drug abusers that needs to be identified before treatment can begin.

PCP in Infants

Symptoms of PCP abuse are also found in the newborn children of women who have used PCP. If a pregnant PCP-user can avoid miscarriage, her newborn will most likely suffer from one, some, or all of the following problems: spinal defects, growth problems, respiratory distress, and blood disorders. Infants also go through withdrawal symptoms, which often include high-pitched crying, irritability, tremors, abnormal eye movement, poor sucking reflexes, poor feeding, listlessness, and diarrhea, as well as poor mental and motor development.[25]

In one test, female rats were injected with PCP on the sixteenth through the twenty-second day of pregnancy. Their pups

The length of time drugs can be detected in the urine

Type of Drug	Average time detectable after ingestion*
Cocaine (metabolite)	2–3 days
Cannabinoids (marijuana) single use Moderate use (4 times per week) Heavy use (daily smoking) Chronic heavy use	3 days 5 days 10 days 21–25 days
Opiates (including heroin, morphine, codeine)	48 hours
Phencyclidine (PCP)**	about 8 days
Amphetamines & methamphetamines	48 hours
Benzodiazepines (including Valium™, Librium™) Therapeutic dose	3 days
Barbiturates Short acting (including secobarbital) Intermediate acting (including phenobarbital) Long acting (including phenobarbital)	24 hours 48–72 hours 7 days or more
Propoxyphene (including Darvon™) Unchanged Metabolite	6 hours 6–48 hours

*Interpretation of the time detectable must take into account many variables such as drug metabolism and half-life, subject's physical condition, fluid balance and state of hydration, route and frequency of ingestion, and testing technique and cutoff level used. These are general guidelines only.

**PCP remains in the body longer than any other street drug, except for marijuana when it is used in heavy or chronically heavy doses.

Sources: American Medical Association, Council on Scientific Affairs, "Scientific issues in drug testing," Journal of American Medical Association (1987), 257(22):3112, table 2, and NIDA, Richard L. Hawks and C. Nora Chiang, eds., Urine testing for drugs of abuse, NIDA Research monograph 73, 1986.

were born seven to eighteen hours after the mother received her last injection. When the brain tissue of the pups was tested, the PCP levels in the brains of the pups was significantly higher than in the mother. The results of this test offer evidence that there is a greater concentration of PCP in the newborn child than in the mother.[26]

In a test of fifty-five infants who went through neonatal withdrawal symptoms, nearly half suffered from temperament problems and a large number never reached the growth size of the average child. Some appear to show the same type of symptoms found in children with cerebral palsy. According to specialists in child abuse and neglect, babies at six months are unduly jittery. At nine months, they cannot understand how their hands work. At a year, their IQs begin to drop, and by two, they cannot form words because their tongues do not work properly. There is evidence that PCP has remained in the blood of children, even at age five, who were born to PCP-dependent mothers.[27]

In a test of two-year olds born to PCP-using mothers, the infants, during their playtime, showed signs of immaturity, attention deficiency, and misbehavior. These children all exhibited marked lower birthweights, shorter lengths, and smaller head sizes.[28] This test suggests that the problems of PCP-infected newborns continue to plague the children as they grow older.

Treatment

PCP hides in the body's fatty tissues and can reappear even though the user believes he or she is free of the drug. Because of this, the treatments used are never foolproof. Even after doctors think that they have rid the user of even the smallest traces of

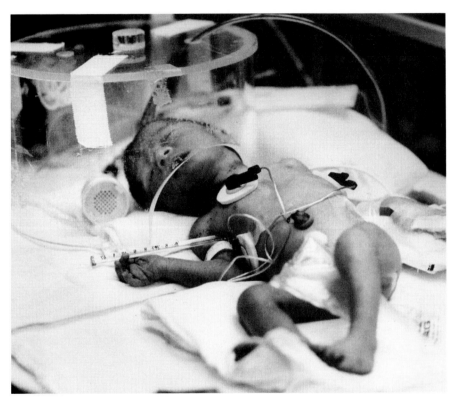

Children born to PCP-dependent mothers will go through withdrawal symptoms at birth. Many of these babies never reach the average size of a non-addicted baby. There is evidence that PCP has remained in the blood of children born to dependent mothers even up until age five.

PCP, symptoms can resurface. Medical experts have, however, classified three levels of detoxification, depending on the extent of PCP abuse.

Stage I—mild intoxication. This stage is generally treated best with comforting support. The user is kept in a quiet place, such as a bed in a darkened room, and given high doses of vitamin C or cranberry juice to acidify the body (raise the acid level) in order to speed the elimination of the drug through the urine. Restraint is used if the patient appears to be in danger of harming himself or herself and because of the possibility of violence; restraint is given only by professionals. Doctors will constantly monitor the patient's vital signs (body temperature, heart rate, pulse, respiration) and check to see if he or she has been unknowingly injured. Patients are often anxious, depressed, and paranoid and exhibit distorted perceptions; some may be hallucinating. "Talking down," a process in which a medical attendant tries to calm the patient by verbally comforting him or her, is not wise because it may agitate the patient even more. If medication is needed, the doctor usually administers some sort of sedative such as Librium™, Valium™, or Haldol™ if the patient shows signs of violence. If the symptoms do not reappear after about twelve hours, the patient is usually discharged.[29]

Stage II—moderate intoxication. This is a more difficult stage to treat. The patient's clothes are loosened. Their bodies are sponged down or rubbed with ice to avoid the onset of unusually high fever known as hyperthermia. In this stage, a urinary catheter is set in place to help eliminate much of the drug trapped in the urine. If the PCP has been ingested or smoked within two hours of treatment, vomiting is induced to clear the stomach. If the drug was taken intravenously or snorted, inducing vomiting serves no purpose. In addition, large doses of activated charcoal may be administered to absorb the PCP in the gastric juices. If PCP was taken more than two hours before hospitalization, a tube placed down the patient's throat is used to suction out its contents. An intravenous tube is inserted to replace the liquids being drained off by the catheter and tracheal tube and to administer doses of dextrose (sugar) and Inderol™, a drug used to control blood pressure. If there is an appearance of muscle rigidity that is not helped by a Valium™ injection, then a neuromuscular block may be necessary. A neuromuscular block is injected directly into the nerve and acts more quickly to reduce muscle rigidity.

Stage III—severe intoxication. This stage may require treatment for convulsions or loss of consciousness in addition to all of the other treatments used in Stages I and II. Moreover, the placement of activated charcoal directly into the stomach may be necessary in order to prevent the intestines from absorbing the PCP as it circulates through the body.[30] The possibility of high blood pressure (hypertension) and heart irregularities (tachycardia) are more serious now. PCP overdose is life threatening because physicians never know if their treatments have rid the body of the poison. As the patient emerges from Stage III symptoms, he or she may also exhibit Stage I or II symptoms. It is not uncommon for patients to become violent or self-destructive as they enter Stage I. Even when the patient is declared clean of PCP, the possibility of brain, liver, lung, or heart diseases may occur. Follow-up sessions with physicians, psychiatrists, psychologists, and social workers are absolutely necessary to help prevent recurrence of problems. It should be noted, however, that almost half the patients who have been treated in psychiatric wards for toxic psychosis begin using PCP again within two weeks after discharge.[31]

The answer to the question of why drug abusers either return to drugs or refuse treatment has really never been answered. But consider the following: Even when offered immediate treatment with no red tape involved, many think that they can manage their drug problem by themselves. Others do not think treatment will be any help. Still others think that going to a treatment center can be humiliating. Moreover, drug abusers often mistakenly think that the drugs are not the problem but the solution.[32] But for those who realize that they now have a chance to begin life anew, a lengthy rehabilitation program, carefully supervised by trained personnel, will begin.

Questions for Discussion

1. If you suspected that a friend was in the early stages of PCP abuse, what would you do to try to ensure that the abuse did not progress?

2. If a friend refused treatment, what might you do to try to convince him or her to stop abusing drugs and go for treatment?

3. What are some alternate activities to drugs that one could engage in for excitement?

4

Drug Abuse and Society

Many factors influence the acceptance or rejection of drug use by society. For instance, the more people who take a drug, the more accepted the drug generally becomes. The more mainstream or middle-class the user, the less of a chance of rejection by society. Recent history has provided us with a good example.

In 1900, tobacco was available to the general public at a reasonable cost. Although the active ingredient in tobacco is a stimulant, nicotine, no one treated the act of cigarette-smoking as a form of drug abuse. During the next fifty years, cigarette-smoking was considered acceptable behavior by both men and women. It was considered sophisticated, so sophisticated that teenagers could not wait until they were old enough to begin smoking.

The sophistication of smoking was reinforced in films and on television in the 1940s and the 1950s. The use of advertising also helped promote smoking. Famous movie stars, as well as respected people in various professions, endorsed certain brands of cigarettes. Some advertisements went so far as to claim that smoking cigarettes helped ease the pain of a sore throat.[1]

In fact, even when a relationship was shown to exist between cigarettes and cancer in the early 1960s, and the Surgeon General enforced the labeling of cigarettes as "Hazardous To Your Health," advertising budgets increased year by year on television ads as well as in print and on outdoor billboards. When it was reported in the early 1970s that second-hand smoke could be dangerous to others, the government and society took a more active role. (Second-hand smoke is what is given off by the cigarette of a smoker and inhaled by others.) Television advertising was banned. Smoking was banned in offices and public buildings. Instead of advertising that promoted the smoking of cigarettes, the government and private organizations such as the American Cancer Society, used advertising to warn consumers of the ill effects of smoking and to convince smokers to give up the habit. Some of the commercials were quite graphic in showing the lungs of a smoker compared to the lungs of a non-smoker.

In a few years, cigarette-smoking was no longer thought to be a sophisticated act but an act of selfishness and ignorance. In fact, cigarette-smokers were likened to drug abusers. They could not get off the habit because the nicotine in tobacco was addictive. The tobacco companies were blamed for knowingly increasing the amount of nicotine in cigarettes to keep smokers coming back for more. Smokers were cut off from society at large. Those who smoked could no longer eat at many restaurants nor find smoking seats on airplanes. Smoking was now a filthy habit. Yet, even as the population of smokers began to decrease, younger people were attracted to smoking perhaps because it was frowned upon by society at large.

When drugs are abused and produce effects in people such as addiction, the effects of addiction are felt by society and government. Unemployment, crime, and the spread of diseases such as tuberculosis, hepatitis B, and AIDS, have changed society's attitudes toward drug use.

At one time, morphine and cocaine were acceptable as medicinal drugs. They were not considered a recreational drug as alcohol was. If people became addicted to these drugs, it was viewed as a personal misfortune, rather than a crime. Once drug abuse and addiction began to increase and addicts were viewed by society with disfavor, laws were passed. The Harrison Narcotic Act of 1914 regulates drug use by stopping its transport throughout the United States. [2]

From 1914 to the late 1950s, more drug laws were enacted. These laws were supported by an educational effort depicting drug abuse as the road to personal ruin. All drug use was seen to be depraved behavior. Those who used drugs were considered degenerates or criminals.[3] During this period, drug use and abuse were largely confined to a subculture of criminals, or the so-called underclass of society.[4]

Addiction was thought to be the result of a personality defect. In 1943, Dr. J.D. Reichard of the federal narcotic farm in Lexington, Kentucky, where drug addicts were treated and/or isolated from society, summarized: "We must never forget that if the poppy plant or marijuana had never been grown [or other] various drugs . . . had never been discovered or synthesized, these people [addicts] would still be problems to someone."[5] He added that as soon as doctors could devise a treatment for the personality defect, the cure and prevention of addiction would be simplified.

On the other hand, Professor Alfred Lindesmith of Indiana University argued as early as 1940 that addiction and drug use were the result of circumstances, peer pressure, curiosity, and associations rather than the result of a personality defect. He said, "There is no evidence to indicate that any personality type [of any social class] is immune to addiction." He thought addiction was largely a reaction to fear of the effects of withdrawal from a drug. His views attained popularity after World War II and into the late 1950s.[6]

In the early 1960s, when the drug LSD was first introduced by the late Dr. Timothy Leary at Harvard University, recreational drug use on college campuses was popular, and first-time drug users were getting younger and younger. It was all thought to be part of growing up in the so-called "Age of Aquarius," or the counterculture (those who claimed that the American middle-class society was too money-oriented, too old, and too inflexible to change). The concept of a "generation gap" between parents and children where each could not communicate with the other was popularized. To be a "flower child" not only meant you wanted peace and love, it often meant you were using drugs. The use of marijuana and experimentation with other drugs like PCP was considered by many people to be romantic and "hip." Cocaine was considered a perfectly safe drug. Magazines, such as *High Times*, described ways to grow marijuana at home, and praised the so-called "virtues" of dropping out and using drugs.[7]

By the early 1970s, drugs entered the mainstream, middle class environment. Rock bands did not hide their drug use. Movies popularized those who lived in a drug culture. Drug use traveled from college campuses back to everyone's neighborhood. The society of America had now fully shifted from subcultures of drug abusers to a drug-using society.

Although there were many people who wanted drugs to be banned because they were dangerous, young drug users discounted this information as the voice of the older generation. Society's reaction was one of frustration. Never before had a younger generation behaved in such a way. Never before had the values of an entire society been questioned and turned upside down. Never before had a war (the war in Vietnam) in which America participated been protested by its youth. In fact, when soldiers began to return from Vietnam, they too became part of the drug culture.

When drug users no longer could get high from their usual dosage of drugs, they began to increase dosages and mix their drugs with others such as PCP. These drugs were beginning to destroy the youth of America.

During the mid-1970s, the abuse of cocaine became an epidemic. It was considered a status drug because of its high cost. It was glamorized by celebrities of the entertainment and sports world. Cocaine was used by doctors, lawyers, and other professionals. In the computer and financial industries, people were not only users of cocaine, they sold the drug in order to maintain their own habits. Drug-dealing and drug use became a problem for the Fortune 500 companies (the top businesses or industries in the country).

Eventually, cocaine would start hitting the streets, but in a different form. It was called crack—a stronger, crystalline form of cocaine that is smoked rather than snorted. It is much less expensive than cocaine, at ten dollars a vial. Crack produced a short but intense high. The high was followed by a severe craving for more of the drug. In the early 1980s, empty crack vials first began appearing on the streets of Los Angeles, Miami, Houston, and Detroit. By 1984, the use of the drug had spread to seventeen major cities, and along with the drug, came the problems of violence and crime.

While the federal government attempted to keep drugs out of the country, getting drugs off the streets became a top priority of local governments. In addition, privately organized neighborhood groups, composed of parents, teachers, and local business people, demanded that drugs be kept off the streets.

Thurman Smith, a parent and resident of a neighborhood in Brooklyn, New York, organized the Ditmas Area Coalition to mobilize against drug dealers. "We've held marches, we've picketed, we've complained to the police . . . so now we're going to do it our way."[8] Along with other parents and residents, Smith identifies drug dealers, takes them to court, and petitions housing agencies to evict drug dealers from public housing.

Local police task forces, such as those in Washington, D.C., and in New York City concentrate their efforts in certain areas, and arrest drug dealers and buyers by the hundreds, confiscating their drugs. In Washington Heights, an area in Manhattan close to the George Washington Bridge, drug dealers selling crack and other illegal drugs, including PCP, were flourishing. Buyers would come from New Jersey, go across the bridge, buy their drugs, and then head back quickly to New Jersey, before they could get caught. New York police began arresting buyers in Washington Heights and impounding their cars. Among those arrested were doctors, lawyers, and even a New Jersey police officer.[9]

Juvenile gang violence began to increase as territorial disputes escalated between gangs who wanted the "privilege and the money for selling drugs."[10] It did not matter if innocent bystanders were killed by rival gangs fighting each other for territory.

Stiff penalties, including jail, were imposed on both drug users and drug dealers. The DEA was given more power to stop large supplies of drugs from entering the United States. There was now a war on drugs. President Ronald Reagan's wife, Nancy, became involved with a "Just Say No" campaign. Many people thought Mrs. Reagan's campaign was "shallow," and "a little silly."[11] They believed "Just Say 'No'" would not have any effect on those smoking crack or snorting cocaine. But Mrs. Reagan's campaign was aimed at millions of young Americans, not at crack and cocaine addicts. In that respect, the campaign may have succeeded. The rate of new young drug abusers did fall in the late 1980s to 1990. The Partnership for a Drug Free America was formed, with funding from both private and government organizations, to create advertisements and educational materials warning people of the dangers of drug abuse.

In 1988, Congress passed a new antidrug bill. It made drugs a national priority by setting up the National Office of Drug Control Policy. It's director, William Bennett, became known as the nation's drug czar.[12] The bill added new powers for the military to stop drugs at the borders of the United States. It also gave law enforcement more authority to arrest criminals. It gave lawyers the power to confiscate major drug dealer's money and assets. It also put defense lawyers of these drug dealers on notice that if their fees were paid with money from drugs they would have to forfeit those fees. Bennett was reinforcing his promise that he would fight the drug wars on all fronts.

MEXICAN MARIJUANA TRAFFICKING TO U.S. CITIES

Washington

California

Colorado

Oklahoma

Texas

Louisiana

Culiacan

Guadalajara

Acapulco

This map shows the major cities in the United States where marijuana from Mexico may eventually end up.

Figures released by the 1994 *Preliminary Estimates from the Drug Abuse Warning Network* show that these efforts initially made some difference, as total drug episodes reported by hospitals went from a high of 425,900 in 1989 to 371,200 in 1990, a decrease of almost 20 percent. But every year thereafter, the numbers began to rise—1994 figures were 508,900 episodes, an increase of 25 percent over four years.[13] Although the messages and measures taken to fight drugs were strong, it appears they have made little difference in the long run. We can conclude that other factors must play a part in these figures.

The Family and The Adolescent

The family is the basic unit of any society. However, according to Karl Zinsmeister of the American Enterprise Institute, "There is a mountain of scientific evidence showing that when families disintegrate, children often end up with intellectual, physical, and emotional scars that persist for life. . . . We talk about the drug crisis . . . [an ill we can] trace back predominantly to one source: broken families."[14] According to the United States Bureau of the Census, the percentage of children living with both biological parents decreased by 22 percent from 1960 to 1991. Conversely, since 1960, the percentage of single-parent families has more than tripled from 9.1 percent to 28.6 percent in 1991.[15] According to William Galston, deputy assistant to President Bill Clinton for domestic policy, and Elaine Kamarck, senior policy advisor to Vice President Al Gore, the absence of a parent in the home can be accompanied by psychological consequences, which include higher than average incidences of youth suicide, mental illness, and drug use.[16]

Children from single-parent households and from households of two working parents are often on their own and therefore spend more time with their peers. Rather than parents providing approval and direction, the adolescent is likely to look to his peer group for approval and direction. If the peer group is one in which drug use is tolerated, it is easy to understand why an adolescent would try drugs, even in the face of tremendous pressure from school and the media not to use drugs. According to the *Index of Leading Cultural Indicators* by William Bennett, two factors, the change in the traditional family and, as a result, the teenager being at risk, may indeed account for the increase in drug use by a younger and younger population.[17]

The Impact of PCP Use

Surveys show that users come from all walks of life. One teenager who appeared on the *Geraldo Show* on March 27, 1996, reported he would "beg, borrow, steal, or do anything I have to" in order to obtain his PCP. When Geraldo Rivera, the host, mentioned the dangerous nature of the drug, the PCP user, said he did not really care. He said that after his mother died he just could not stand living with his crazy father, so he lived on the streets. He mentioned that it was great to feel as if he could do anything, and that was the reason why he needed to have PCP.[18]

The "Typical" PCP User

Analysts use two methods to determine the profile of a "typical" PCP user. They do a demographic profile (similar to the style of the U.S. Census), which is concerned largely with classifying people according to the following categories:

- Age—According to the survey, ages can be grouped in a variety of ways. In using the figures from the 1994 *National Household Survey on Drug Abuse*, age groups are classified from twelve through seventeen, eighteen through twenty-five, twenty-six through thirty-four, and thirty-five and older.

- Gender—Male and female

- Race—White, Black, Hispanic, Asian

Additional categories that can be used in demographic surveys include:

- Income—Total by household

- Education

- Employment Status

    Employed (full time, part time)

    Unemployed

- Profession

- Region in the United States

The psychographic profile is another kind of survey. This kind of profile is more concerned with the attitudes and opinions of certain groups of people. Surveys, used during election campaigns, those used by advertising agencies, for instance, to determine what people think about a particular candidate or particular products, are considered psychographic surveys.

The National Household Survey on Drug Abuse uses both

demographic and psychographic methods for their profiles. The most recent survey revealed the following information:

- In 1994, there were approximately 12.6 million Americans classified as illicit drug users. This means they had used an illegal drug the month before the interview.

- The rate of illegal drug use in 1994 was highest among young adults, eighteen to twenty-one years old (15.2 percent) and youth, sixteen to seventeen years old (14.5 percent).

- Most illegal drug-users were white. (76 percent of all users). Blacks accounted for 14 percent of all users, and Hispanics accounted for 8 percent of all users.

- Males (at 7.9 percent) have a higher rate of current illegal drug use than females (at 4.3 percent). In the twelve to seventeen age group, the rate of male to female use is more equal, with the male rate at 8.5 percent and the female rate at 7.8 percent.

- Illegal drug use shows a clear relationship to years of education completed. Among males, eighteen to thirty-four, those who had not finished high school had the highest rate of drug use (14.6 percent), and college graduates had the lowest rate (6.7 percent).

- Another relationship is demonstrated between illegal drug use and employment. Of illegal drug users, 13.9 percent of adults were unemployed compared with 6.7 percent of employed adults.

- The western region of the United States had the highest rate of drug abusers (6.6 percent) compared to the Northeast (5.1 percent).

Since marijuana is the drug most closely associated with PCP, it is interesting to note that marijuana is the most commonly used drug (81 percent) by all drug users. Furthermore, 20 percent of all drug users said they used marijuana only in combination with another drug. This would appear to confirm that PCP is used more frequently than statistics would suggest.[19] According to preliminary estimates of the Drug Abuse Warning Network (DAWN), PCP-related emergency episodes in hospitals in 1994 increased to 6,000 from a low of 3,500 in 1991.[20]

These figures appear to confirm that illegal drug abuse, in general, remains a continual problem and that PCP abuse, in particular, is increasing.

The psychographic survey contained information that was far more troubling for young people, ages twelve to seventeen. Two of the measures the *National Household Survey* uses to predict how serious a drug problem is within a certain group are the attitude the user has about the risk of harm when taking the drug and how easily available the drug is for the user to obtain. The analysts showed that in groups where the risk of harm for using a drug was thought to be high, drug use was less. If the group thought there was less risk of harm when using a drug, drug use was higher. Additionally, if the group thought the drug was easily available to them, drug use was higher than if the group thought the drug was hard to get.

- In the twelve to seventeen age group, the percentage of those surveyed who believed using marijuana

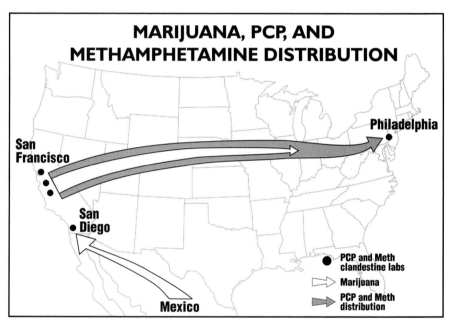

MARIJUANA, PCP, AND METHAMPHETAMINE DISTRIBUTION

Philadelphia

San Francisco

San Diego

Mexico

● PCP and Meth clandestine labs

▷ Marijuana

➤ PCP and Meth distribution

This map shows some of the most common cities in the United States where marijuana, PCP, and methamphetamines from Mexico are distributed.

posed a great risk of harm, dropped from 49.8 percent in 1992 to 42.0 percent in 1994.

• In that same age group, the percentage of those who believed using PCP posed a great risk of harm, dropped from 47.8 percent in 1992 to 43.2 percent in 1994. It is interesting to note in both cases that less than half of those in the twelve to seventeen age group, think there is great harm in using either marijuana or PCP.[21]

• Between 1992 and 1994, the percentage of those in the twelve to seventeen age group who believed that marijuana and PCP, or combinations of both, were easily available increased from 51 percent in 1992 to 58.7 percent in 1994.[22]

In summary, two important factors appear to account for increased drug use in the twelve to seventeen age group. The group's attitude toward the relative danger of the drug and the availability of the drug were both factors in its use. In both cases, fewer and fewer members of the twelve to seventeen age group believe there is danger in using drugs, particularly marijuana and PCP. Within that same age group, more and more members believe these drugs are easy to obtain.

Now that you have all these statistics, you must keep something else in mind. These statistics may be under-reported. The surveys, for the most part, were conducted in people's homes and in hospitals. But what about the countless drug abusers who live in the streets, in shelters, or in rehabilitation centers? How about the drug abusers who have dropped out of school? Chances are these groups were not polled. The abuse problem is an issue shared by all races, all sexes, all regions. The condition is probably far worse than the polls reflect.[23]

The Young Lady in Detroit

In August 1995, Deletha Word, a young woman who lived in Detroit, was driving home from a popular beach area into the city. According to witnesses, she was speeding. She crashed into a car driven by Martel Welch, a six-foot-three nineteen-year-old former high school football player. Word sped away from the accident. Welch got out of his car, looked at the damage, got back into the car, and chased after Word. He finally was able to stop her on a bridge that connected the beach area to the city. He got out of his car, approached Word's car, and received no response as he began yelling at her. He said she appeared to be "on another planet." Finally, he had enough of her bizarre behavior. He dragged her out of her car and began to hit her. A crowd was forming and watching as Word tried to get away from Welch. They battled so hard, Welch ripped the T-shirt off Word. Barely clothed, Word ran down the bridge, away from Welch. Then she turned and ran in the opposite direction, with Welch still behind her. The size of the crowd was increasing. There was a great deal of screaming. Finally, Word climbed a bridge barrier. She saw Welch approach her. He yelled, "Don't jump!" Word jumped or fell off the bridge. No one will ever know if her action was accidental or on purpose, but Word drowned.

The police arrived, and Welch was arrested, charged with murder. The case was tried April 18, 1996, and televised on *Court TV*.[24] Martel Welch's defense was that he did not murder Deletha Word. His attorney said he would prove Word was high on PCP and that was the reason why she jumped from the bridge.

The trial took many days. Through questioning, it was revealed that Deletha Word was a drug abuser who had started

A "burned out" user will become spacey—impossible to understand, unable to think clearly, or remember things. Some users remain depressed, moody, and confused for as long as a year.

using drugs at the age of thirteen. She used many drugs, but her drugs of choice were marijuana, cocaine, and PCP. According to her hospital records, she had been a chronic abuser of PCP for more than five years. Her mother testified that her daughter was uncoordinated. In fact, she had recently been released from one hospital that had treated her because she dropped a butcher knife on her foot while at home, causing considerable damage. Her mother said she did not know what she would do with her. She said that from one day to the next her behavior would change. Deletha was hospitalized many times because her mother was afraid she would hurt herself. Additional hospital records revealed that she had tried to commit suicide more than once. As far as Deletha Word's mother was concerned, there was nothing further she could do to help her daughter except to hospitalize her as often as she could.

At the end of the trial, the jurors had to determine whether the beatings and threatening displays of Martel Welch caused Deletha Word to jump off the bridge or whether Deletha Word was just reacting to the effects of her PCP use. After deliberating for two days, the jury convicted Martel Welch of murder. They said that although PCP abuse was a contributing factor in Deletha Word's disorientation, if Martel Welch had not been on the scene, chances are Word would not have jumped off the bridge.

No matter how the jury voted, in this particular case, you could conclude that PCP abuse produced some far-reaching effects. Not only was Deletha Word a victim, so was Martel Welch. He would be spending most of his life in jail. Word's mother, also a victim, lost her daughter.

Questions for Discussion

1. Name some of the reasons that drug abuse is not considered socially acceptable in society today.

2. Do you think that the "Just Say No" approach to drugs is an effective method of prevention. Why? Why not?

3. Do you think there is any way of reaching the vast numbers of drug abusers who are never counted in official surveys? What methods would you suggest?

5

The Family and PCP

Reggie Davis (not his real name) began drinking at age seven and continued drinking on and off during junior high school. He thought it was easy to get away with because his father always kept beer in the refrigerator and never noticed when a few cans were missing. Reggie thought it would be even easier to swipe hard liquor from his parent's bar. He knew no one really kept track because his parents and their friends entertained themselves almost every other weekend. At school, Reggie would hide small bottles of vodka in his locker. Even though Reggie's friends knew what he was doing, no one said anything. Reggie thought to himself, "These kids must think I'm cool!"

By the time he was in high school, Reggie was into marijuana. In his junior year, he was reprimanded for dozing off in school. Reggie's parents were aware his behavior had changed at home.

He was often hostile. If his parents asked any questions, Reggie would turn on them in a rage. Finally, all three went to a family therapy center. The counselor told the Davises that Reggie's change in behavior was probably a phase he was going through and it would soon pass. The counselor never asked Reggie about alcohol or drugs. Reggie's parents never asked about drug use either. They were satisfied that Reggie would outgrow this phase. Perhaps they did not want to know any more.

One night, Reggie tried something new: marijuana laced with PCP. At 1:00 A.M. Reggie ran through the house screaming. He woke his parents. He thought his father, who had come running out, was the devil. Reggie ran to the kitchen to get a knife to protect himself. Mr. Davis had a difficult time trying to dodge Reggie's lunges in order to get the knife out of his hand. Mrs. Davis recalled that it seemed to her to be like a scene out of a bad movie. She was screaming while Mr. Davis wrestled Reggie to the floor. Then she called an ambulance. Reggie's parents took him to a hospital.

He was observed as the drugs left his body over a period of several hours. Later, because Reggie and his parents would not answer questions about what had happened to cause this behavior, Reggie was admitted to the psychiatric ward of the hospital.

Having had to face close calls before, Reggie convinced his parents as well as the hospital staff that he had just started using drugs. "No more PCP for me," he said to himself, "No more drugs for me," he promised his parents. They all wanted to believe him. They had him released to home. The Davises believed the nightmare was over. But for them, Reggie, and for his sister, Wendy, the nightmare was just beginning.

The next year found Reggie and his family drifting apart.

Reggie continued his use of PCP. But no longer could the family sit down to dinner together. There were too many confrontations and too many broken dishes. Reggie's parents rarely left the house and stopped seeing most of their friends. They never knew when Reggie would become uncontrollable.

Reggie continued to attend school but only to meet his new friends, who provided the acceptance he was not getting at home. Wendy, Reggie's younger sister, sobbed "Why can't we be like normal people? I hate Reggie. I hate what he's done to us." Mr. Davis began working later and later hours in order to avoid the tensions at home. Reggie's mom began taking tranquilizers to calm her nerves. The entire household revolved around Reggie's PCP abuse. "We can't even talk about the weather or sports," Mr. Davis said. "How can we, when everyday our son is destroying himself?" Both parents tried to determine where they had gone wrong. They tried to be stern with Reggie and not give him any money. But he would leave the house and not come back for hours or days.

He once played the stereo so loud for twenty-four hours, that he was almost arrested. His parents spoke to the police, and the incident was forgotten. The Davis family was making excuses for everything Reggie did. But when Wendy started to have problems in school and became withdrawn, Reggie's parents had had enough. They could not bear losing another child. They admitted Reggie to a psychiatric hospital, where Reggie finally admitted how out of control he was. Reggie had to undergo a treatment program and live full-time at the treatment center.[1]

It is clear that when there is an abuse problem with one child, all family members suffer. Steps must be taken by everyone in the family to recognize the problem and do something about it. It

Some PCP users have found themselves in violent conditions, forcing police to arrest them, often for their own safety.

took Reggie's parents more than a year to admit to themselves the extent of Reggie's problem. Although they knew Reggie's problems were due to drug abuse, they were helpless to cure him. A professional would have to do that. First, however, Reggie had to make the decision to stop.

Reggie's family was involved from the very beginning of his treatment. The Davis family learned about chemical dependency and drug abuse in its various stages, with specific emphasis on PCP. In some sessions Reggie's family met with Reggie's friends, teachers, and cousins, to learn how they felt. While all agreed they cared about Reggie, they all admitted they were angry and resentful about the damage he caused. After a few more sessions, they met with Reggie and confronted him with their feelings. "You stole money from me to get high," claimed his best friend. "You lied to me about your father being ill so you would be excused from a full term's worth of work . . . I don't know that I can ever trust you again," his teacher lamented. "You made mommy and daddy so crazy, they forgot I was alive," Wendy cried. All these accusations made Reggie angry, but by the end of the session he began to realize the enormity of his abuse problem and to what extent it had affected the people he most loved.

After a few weeks, Reggie was asked to write about his feelings toward his family. The Davises did the same. After reading each other's words, they went through a process called "amends," in which each person says what he or she is most sorry for doing.[2]

"I'm sorry I never told you how much I loved you," Mr. Davis admitted. "Why didn't you tell me before?" Reggie asked. Mr. Davis explained that he thought Reggie would understand because he could see how much his father did for him. "Would I do that much for you if I didn't love you?" he said. Mr. Davis and Reggie embraced for the first time in three years.

During the second phase of Reggie's treatment, he had to learn how to live without drugs. In the third phase, he had to prepare to rejoin the community. He had to live with another family whose child had abused drugs. In conversations with that family, he began to fully understand the feelings of helplessness his parents must have had.

Finally, Reggie was allowed to go home. But some changes had been made. The Davises no longer kept alcohol at home and stopped drinking themselves. They continued to attend a support group for parents. The Davises were now communicating with each other regularly instead of keeping everything bottled up inside. Mrs. Davis said, "Before we were a bunch of unhappy people living at the same address. Now we are a family."[3]

According to Barbara Vobejda, in her 1992 *Washington Post* article, families that communicate the way the Davises now do are not so easy to find. Teenagers spend an average of three hours per day in front of the television, compared to an average of five minutes per day they spend alone with their fathers and twenty minutes with their mothers.[4]

In an annual survey of two hundred thousand junior and senior high school students, the National Parents' Resource Institute for Drug Education (PRIDE) reported that 34 percent of students said their parents talk to them frequently about the dangers of drug abuse. That is one-third of the parents, and the figure is down from 39 percent in 1991–92. Thirty-three percent said their parents do not set clear rules, and 50 percent said they are not disciplined when rules are broken. The study did show that parental and family communication and involvement could

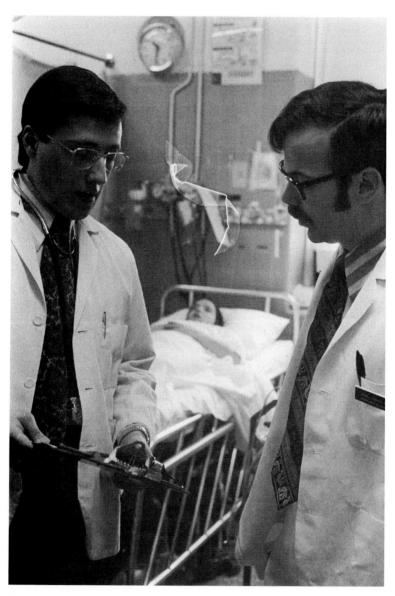

Though doctors may think that they have rid the user of every trace of PCP in his or her system, symptoms can reappear. Even after PCP use has been stopped, a long rehabilitation program, properly supervised by trained personnel, is often necessary.

help prevent drug use just as it helped the Davis family in supporting Reggie during his drug rehabilitation.[5]

Current research indicates there is no typical "PCP Family." Families can be rich, middle class, or poor. There are some indications that PCP use has spread to rural areas, but urban and suburban families are most often the victims of a PCP drug-user in the family. Two-parent families are not immune from the effects of drug abuse either. Although more PCP abusers may live in families where there is a single parent as head of the household, there are many who come from traditional two-parent families. Families should never feel safe enough to dismiss the idea of a PCP user living with them.

Watching for Danger Signs

One step the family as a whole can take to deal with potential drug abuse is to become better educated. This will help them to recognize the potential signs of drug abuse in a member of the family. That recognition must be followed by open communication and trust within the family. The following are some of the danger signs that a family member or friend may be using drugs:

- The user has new friends who you suspect are using drugs.

- The user is doing poorly in school for the first time.

- Activities such as sports, music, or baby-sitting are no longer preferred.

- Moodiness, fatigue, and depression have taken the place of happiness.

- Trouble in sleeping occurs.

- The user does not seem to care anymore about how he or she looks.

- Lack of appetite and weight loss are apparent.

- Sudden mood shifts take place, from seeming fairly okay to being extremely angry or nervous.

Parents and siblings should be concerned if they notice one or more of these changes.[6]

Questions for Discussion

1. If you suspected that a member of your family had a drug problem what would you do to try to help that person?

2. If you or someone you know had a problem with drugs and could not talk to a family member, who else could you suggest?

3. Suggest some ways of opening the lines of communication between family members.

Where to Go for Help

There are many organizations that can help educate a family before a drug problem occurs. Elementary, middle, and high schools provide information to their students about the dangers of drug abuse. Often a drug counselor is part of the school staff, and he or she can become instrumental in warning a family that there is a potential drug problem with one of its members. School personnel are often the first to recognize a problem. If a student who ordinarily does well in school begins to fail, or if he or she starts missing school on a regular basis, this may be hidden from the family, but not from school personnel. School counselors and teachers are familiar with, and can direct the family to, sources of information and assistance within the community. If a community is large enough, it will support at least one drug abuse program or a chapter of Families Anonymous. Families Anonymous is just one of many organizations that can provide support and direction to family members. Usually there are other families who are involved with drug abusers who can offer encouragement and ways to cope that they have learned from their own experiences. It helps for families to know they are not alone.

What families learn is to put the responsibility for a child's drug abuse on that child's shoulders. They learn that they must let go of actions they can no longer control and take actions that preserve the family first. If the problem is severe enough, the family may have to send the child to an institution where the child is treated for the side effects of drug withdrawal. The family may also enter group therapy.

Private counseling and participation in a group with other concerned people who have a drug abuser in the family can help. Finally, it is important to understand that drug abusers may not have the motivation to benefit from all the professional service that is needed. Parents and siblings should not give up. They should feel good about making every resource available to drug abusers, but they cannot force an abuser to benefit from it.

REFERRAL SOURCES

The following are lists of resources available to families nationwide for educational and support services.

FEDERAL AGENCIES

The Office of Alcohol and Substance Abuse Prevention
Department of the Interior
Washington, DC (202) 208-6188

Center for Substance Abuse Prevention Workplace,
(800) 843-4971 9:00 A.M. – 8:00 P.M. E.S.T.

Center for Substance Abuse Treatment (CSAT)
A Division of Substance Abuse and Mental Health Services Administration (SAMHSA) Rockville, MD (800) 662-HELP

Corporation for National Service Drug Alliance Office
(formerly ACTION)
Washington, DC (202) 606-5000

Drug Czar's Office
Office of National Drug Control Policy
Executive Office of the President
Washington, DC
(202) 395-6700

Drug Information and Strategy Clearinghouse
Washington, DC
(800) 578-3472

Drugs and Crime Clearinghouse
Rockville, MD
(800) 666-3332
e-mail: askncjrs @ncjrs.aspensys.com

Indian Health Service
Alcoholism and Substance Abuse Program
Rockville, MD
(301) 443-4297

Juvenile Justice Clearinghouse
Washington, DC
(800) 638-8736 (8:30 A.M. - 7:00 P.M. EST)

National AIDS Clearinghouse
Rockville, MD
(800) 458-5231

National Clearinghouse for Alcohol and Drug Abuse Information (NCADI)
Rockville, MD
(800) 729-6686

National Institute on Alcohol Abuse and Alcoholism (NIAAA)
Prevention Research Branch
Rockville, MD
(301) 443-1677

Office for Women's Services
Rockville, MD
(301) 443-5184

NATIONAL ORGANIZATIONS
The Advocacy Institute
(Media advocacy and smoking control issues)
Washington, DC
(202) 659-8475

African-American Family Services
(formerly Institute on Black Chemical Abuse)
Minneapolis, MN
(612) 871-7878

American Council for Drug Education (ACDE)
Rockville, MD
(800) 488-DRUG

Center on Addiction and Substance Abuse
Columbia University (CASA)
New York, NY
(212) 841-5200

Clearinghouse on Child Abuse and Neglect Information
Chicago, IL
(800) 394-3366

Committees of Correspondence, Inc.
(Drug prevention resources)
Danvers, MA
(508) 774-2641

Community Anti-Drug Coalitions of America (CADCA)
Alexandria, VA
(703) 706-0560

CWD International, Inc.
(Drug and violence prevention)
Pittsburgh, PA
(412) 731-8019

Drug Abuse Resistance Education (DARE)
Los Angeles, CA
(800) 223-DARE

Drug Watch International
Elmhurst, IL
(708) 550-8999

ELKS Drug Awareness Program
(Emphasis on "gateway" drugs)
Ashland, OR
(503) 482-3193

Family Resource Coalition
Chicago, IL
(312) 341-0900

International Institute on Inhalant Abuse
Englewood, CO
(303) 788-4617

Join Together
A National Resource for Communities Fighting Substance Abuse
Boston, MA
(617) 437-1500

Just Say No International
Oakland, CA
(800) 258-2766

Life Education Center
(Affiliate of Drug Watch International)
Elmhurst, IL
(708) 530-8999

Narcotics Anonymous (NA) World Service Office
Van Nuys, CA
(888) 332-6362 (toll-free)

National Asian Pacific American Families Against Substance Abuse, Inc. (NAPAFASA)
Los Angeles, CA
(213) 278-0031

National Association for Families
Addiction Research and Education
Chicago, IL
(312) 541-1272

National Association for Native American Children of Alcoholics
Seattle, WA
(800) 322-5601

National Association of Community Partnerships
Mankato, MN
(507) 387-5643

National Association of Prevention Professionals and Advocates, Inc. (NAPPA)
Chicago, IL
(312) 378-2432

National Association of State Alcohol and Drug Abuse Directors (NASADAD)
Washington, DC
(202) 783-6868

National Association on Drug Abuse Problems (NADAP)
New York, NY
(212) 986-1170

National Black Alcoholism and Addictions Council,
Washington, DC
(202) 296-2696

National Coalition of Hispanic Health and Human Services Organization
Washington, DC
(202) 387-5000

National Coalition to Prevent Impaired Driving (NCPID)
Washington, DC
(202) 659-0054

National Commission Against Drunk Driving (NCADD)
Washington, DC
(202) 452-6004

National Council on Alcoholism and Drug Dependence, Inc. (NCADD)
New York, NY
(800) NCA-CALL

National Crime Prevention Council (NCPC)
Washington, DC
(202) 466-NCPC

**National Families in Action
(NFIA)**
Atlanta, GA
(770) 934-6364

National Family Partnership (NFP)
Communication headquarters
St. Louis, MO
(314) 845-1933

National Inhalant Prevention Coalition
Austin, TX
(800) 269-4237

National Rural Alcohol and Drug Abuse Network, Inc.
University of Wisconsin
Troy, WI
(715) 836-3990

National Women's Health Network
Washington, DC
(202) 347-1140

**Parents Resource Institute for Drug Education
(PRIDE)**
Atlanta, GA
(770) 458-9900

Partnership for a Drug-Free America
New York, NY
(212) 922-1560

Resource Center on Substance Abuse Prevention and Disability
Washington, DC
(202) 628-8080

ToughLove International
Doylestown, PA
(800) 333-1069

Youth-to-Youth
Columbus, OH
(614) 224-4506

Chapter Notes

Introduction

1. Richard Allen, "4 days out of the Mental Clinic, Mugger Shot," *Brooklyn Paper*, January 1996, p. 1.
2. Eric Hedegaard, "Up Against the Wahlberg," *Details*, April 1996, p. 120.
3. George Rush and Joanna Molloy, "A 'Titanic' dustup leaves crew reeling," *New York Daily News*, September 8, 1996, p. 14.
4. "James Brown's Wife Died After Taking PCP and Prescription Drugs, Autopsy Report Says," *Jet*, February 26, 1996, p. 18.
5. "James Brown's Wife Arrested on Drug Charge Third Time," *Jet*, June 6, 1988, p. 52.
6. Michael Goldberg, "James Brown Addicted to PCP," *Rolling Stone*, November 17, 1988, p. 42.
7. Penny Konlyn, *Real Facts—The Truth About Drugs* (Circle Pines, Minn.: American Guidance Service, 1989), p. 51.

Chapter 1

1. Lynette Holloway, "Queens Woman is Found Guilty of Killing 2 Priests in Car Crash," *The New York Times*, March 22, 1995, p. B3.
2. U.S. Department of Health and Human Services, *Preliminary Estimates from the Drug Abuse Warning Network*, Advance Report #11, Rockville, Md., November 1995, p. 18.
3. David W. Maurer and Victor H. Vogel, *Narcotics and Narcotics Addiction* (Springfield, Ill.: Thomas, 1967), p. 5.
4. Richard Seymour, David Smith, Darryl Inaba, and Mim Landry, *The New Drugs: Look-Alikes, Drugs of Deception and Designer Drugs* (Center City, Minn.: Hazelden Foundation, 1989), p. 27.
5. Ibid.
6. Maurer and Vogel, p. 4.

7. Seymour et al., p. 5.
8. Ibid., pp. 32–33.
9. Maurer and Vogel, p. 144.
10. Seymour et al., pp. 6–7.
11. Maurer and Vogel, p. 6.
12. Ibid., p. 8.
13. Seymour et al., p. 25.
14. Ibid., pp. 33–34.
15. *The Chris Mathews Show*, CNBC, April, 10, 1995.

Chapter 2

1. Brent Q. Hafen and Kathryn J. Frandsen, *PCP Phencyclidine "Angel Dust"* (Center City, Minn.: Hazelden Foundation, 1988), p. 3.

2. V. Harold Maddox, "The Historical Development of Phencyclidine," in *PCP (Phencyclidine): Historical and Current Perspectives*, ed. Edward F. Domino (Ann Arbor, Mich.: NPP Books, 1981), p. 4.

3. Hafen and Frandsen, pp. 3–4.

4. Tom McNichol, "PCP, The Cheap Thrill with a High Price," *Rolling Stone*, March 24, 1988, p. 85.

5. Hafen and Frandsen, p. 4.

6. Thomas J. Young, "PCP Use Among Adolescents," *Child Study Journal*, vol. 17, no. 1, 1987, p. 57.

7. National Educational Foundation of America, *Phencyclidine-PCP-Peace Pill*, June 20, 1991. p. 1.

8. Hafen and Fransden, p. 5.

9. Florence Isaacs, "Angel Dust—The Unpredictable Killer," *Readers Digest*, Vol. 113, September 1978, pp. 127–128.

10. McNichol, p. 84.

11. Preliminary estimates from the 1994 National Household Survey on Drug Abuse, U.S. Department of Health and Human Services, Rockville, Md., 1995, p. 5.

12. Ovid Isaacs, Paul Martin, and James A. Washington, Jr., "Phencyclidine (PCP) Abuse," *Oral Surgery, Oral Medicine, Oral Pathology*, February 1986, p. 126.

13. McNichol, p. 84.

14. Substance Abuse and Mental Health Services Administration, *Drug Abuse Warning Network*, Rockville, Md., April 1995, p. 50.

15. Christopher S. Wren, "60's Drug Is Back, Police Say as They Announce Arrests," *The New York Times*, April 12, 1996, p. B4.

16. Isaacs, p. 130.

17. Ibid., p. 128.

18. Michele McCormick, *Designer Drug Abuse* (New York: Franklin Watts, 1989), p. 62.

19. Diane K. Beebe and Elizabeth Walley, "Substance Abuse: The Designer Drugs," *American Family Physician*, May 1991, p. 1693.

20. John Larabee, "Marijuana's Rise in Popularity Among Youths is Tied to Easy Access," *Detroit News*, January 10, 1996, p. 5D.

21. McNichol, pp. 173–174.

22. McCormick, p. 80.

23. Bill Rankin, "Ex-student Convicted in PCP Drug Case," *Atlanta Journal Constitution*, July 16, 1994, p. B6.

24. Drug Enforcement Administration, *The Supply of Illicit Drugs in the United States*, August 1995, *National Narcotics Intelligence Consumers' Committee Report*, http://www.usdoj.gov/dea

25. M.M. Kirsch, *Designer Drugs* (Minneapolis, Minn.: CompCare Publications, 1986), p. 155.

26. Ibid.

27. Mary H. Cooper, *The Business of Drugs* (Washington, D.C.: The Congressional Quarterly, 1990), p. 91.

28. McNichol, p. 84.

29. Kirsch, p. 145.

30. Kirsch, p. 144.

31. *ABC News*, New York, February 12, 1997.

32. Carroll, pp. 81–82.

33. U.S Department of Justice, Drug Enforcement Administration, *Drugs of Abuse* (Arlington, Va.: U.S. Department of Justice, 1996), p. 8.

34. "2 Leaders of PCP Convicted." *Los Angeles Times*, February 16, 1996, p. B6.

Chapter 3

1. Brent Q. Hafen and Kathryn J. Frandsen, *PCP, Phencyclidine, "Angel Dust"* (Center City, Minn.: Hazeldon Foundation, 1988), p. 12.

2. Joel Engel, *Addicted: Kids Talking about Drugs in Their Own Words* (New York: Tom Doherty Associates, Inc., 1989), p. 159.

3. Ed., Harvey W. Feldman and Dan Waldorf, *Angel Dust in Four American Cities: An Ethnographic Study of PCP Abusers* (Rockville, Md.: U.S. Department of Health and Human Services, National Institute on Drug Abuse Services Research Report (ADM) 81–1039, 1980), p. 9.

4. Thomas Milhorn, Jr., "Diagnosis and Management of Phencyclidine Intoxication," in *American Family Physician*, April 1991, pp. 1296–1297.

5. Florence Isaacs, "Angel Dust—The Unpredictable Killer," *Reader Digest*, Vol. 113, September 1978, p. 129.

6. Tom McNichol, "PCP, The Cheap Thrill With a High Price," *Rolling Stone*, March 24, 1988, p. 84.

7. Carroll, p. 20.

8. Lawrence Clayton, *Designer Drugs* (New York: Rosen, 1994), p. 12.

9. Richard G. Schlaadt and Peter T. Shannon, *Drugs of Choice*, 2nd ed. (New York: Prentice Hall, 1986), p. 211.

10. Timothy W. Kinlock, "Does Phencyclidine (PCP) Use Increase Violent Crime?" *Journal of Drug Issues*, vol. 21, Fall 1991, pp. 797–799.

11. Isaacs, pp. 127–129.

12. Thomas J. Young, "PCP Use Among Adolescents," *Child Study Journal*, vol. 17, no. 1, pp. 57–59.

13. Brian R. Ward, *The Brain and Nervous System* (New York: Franklin Watts, 1984), pp. 18–23.

14. Milhorn, p. 1295.

15. Ovid Isaacs, Paul Martin and James A. Washington, Jr., "Phencyclidine (PCP) Abuse," *Oral Surgery, Oral Medicine, Oral Pathology*, February 1986, p. 128.

16. *American Heritage Dictionary*, 2nd college ed., (Boston: Houghton Mifflin Company, 1982), pp. 1000, 1282.

17. Young, p. 58.

18. Carroll, p. 50.

19. Florence Isaacs, " Angel Dust—The Unpredictable Killer," *Readers Digest*, vol. 113, September 1978, p.129.

20. Young, p. 58.

21. Carroll, p. 46.

22. Ibid., p. 50.

23. Ibid., pp. 47–48.

24. Ibid., p. 59.

25. Hafen and Frandsen, p. 15.

26. Frederick K. Goodwin, "Phencyclidine and Pregnancy," *Journal of the American Medical Association*, vol. 262, no. II., September 15, 1989, p. 1439.

27. Kirsch, pp. 152–153.

28. Leila Beckwith, Carol Redning, Deborah Morris and Leslie Phillipson, "Spontaneous Play in Two-year-olds Born to Substance Abusing Mothers," *Infant Mental Health Journal*, vol. 15, Summer 1994, , pp. 199–201.

29. Miller, p. 217.

30. Kirsch, p. 150.

31. Carroll, p. 67.

32. Elliot Currie, *Reckoning: Drugs, the Cities, and the American Future* (New York: Hill and Wang, 1993), p. 230.

Chapter 4

1. David W. Maurer and Victor H. Vogel, *Narcotics and Narcotics Addiction* (Springfield, Ill.: Thomas, 1967), p. 11.

2. Richard Seymour, David Smith, Darryl Inaba, and Mim Landry, *The New Drugs: Look Alikes, Drugs of Deception and Designer Drugs* (Center City, Minn.: Hazelden Foundation, 1989), p. 23.

3. Maurer and Vogel, pp. 19–20.

4. Ibid., p. 26

5. H. Wayne Morgan, *Drugs In America: A Social History, 1800–1980* (Syracuse, N.Y.: Syracuse University Press, 1981), p. 132.

6. Ibid, p. 133.

7. Seymour et al., p. 29.

8. Thomas and Dorothy Hoobler, *Drugs and Crime* (New York: Chelsea House Publishers, 1988), p. 109.

9. Ibid., p. 106

10. Ibid., p. 107.

11. Michael Kronenwetter, *Drugs in America: The Users, the Suppliers, the War on Drugs* (Englewood Cliffs, N.J.: Messner, 1990), p. 88.

12. Ibid.

13. U.S. Department of Health and Human Services, *Preliminary Estimates from the Drug Abuse Warning Network,* Advance Report #11, November 1995, p. 48.

14. William J. Bennett, *The Index of Leading Cultural Indicators* (New York: Simon & Schuster, 1994), p. 45.

15. Ibid., p. 50.

16. Ibid., p. 54.

17. Ibid.

18. "Teenage Street People," *Geraldo*, CBS-TV, March 27, 1966.

19. U.S. Department of Health and Human Services, *Preliminary Estimates from the 1994 National Household Survey on Drug Abuse*, Advance Report # 10, pp. 18–19.

20. Ibid., p. 18.

21. Ibid., p. 16.

22. Ibid., p. 17.

23. Ibid.

24. "*Welch* vs. *Detroit*," *Court TV*, April 18–25, 1996.

Chapter 5

1. Diane Hales, *Case Histories* (New York: Chelsea House, 1987), pp. 26–29

2. Ibid., p.30.

3. Ibid., p. 31.

4. William J. Bennett, *The Index of Leading Cultural Indicators* (New York: Simon and Schuster, 1994), p. 103

5. *Drugs: What Every Parent Should Know* (New York: United Federation of Teachers, 1992), unpaged.

6. William L. LaFountain, *Setting Limits: Parents, Kids and Drugs* (Center City, Minn.: Hazelden Foundation, 1982), p. 10.

Glossary

addiction—A condition caused by repeated drug use in which the user feels that he or she cannot stop using the drug or must increase the dosage. The user becomes physiologically and/or psychologically dependent on the drug.

amphetamine—Any one of a number of drugs that act to stimulate parts of the central nervous system.

analgesic—A medication that reduces or eliminates pain.

analogs—Drugs that are similar variations of other drugs.

anesthetic—A substance used to eliminate the sensation of pain, often causing a person to become unconscious.

anxiety—A state of distress, worry, or uneasiness.

axon—A long thread extending from the body of a neuron along which a single message is carried.

barbiturate—Any one of a number of drugs that are used to relieve anxiety by causing a depression of the central nervous system.

central nervous system—Essentially the brain and the spinal chord.

cocaine—A colorless or white crystalline narcotic extracted from the leaves of the coca plant. Cocaine can be both a stimulant and an anesthetic.

codeine—A depressant drug derived from opium.

Controlled Substances Act (CSA)—A law enacted in 1979 designed to control the manufacture, sale, and use of potentially dangerous drugs.

crack—A less expensive, highly addictive form of cocaine.

dendrites—The finely branched endings of a nerve cell that transmit impulses toward the cell body.

Drug Abuse Warning Network (DAWN)—An organization that monitors trends in drug use and abuse in the United States.

Drug Enforcement Administration (DEA)—United States federal agency in the Justice Department formed in 1973 to monitor the sale and distribution of legal and illegal drugs.

ether—A highly flammable liquid composed of oxygen, carbon, and hydrogen and widely used as an anesthetic.

flashback—The return of hallucinogenic images after the immediate effects of a hallucinogen have worn off.

hallucinogen—Any drug that produces sensory impressions, or visions that have no basis in reality.

heroin—A highly addictive, white, odorless crystalline narcotic made from morphine.

Lysergic acid diethylamide (LSD)—A hallucinogenic drug commonly called "acid" that is derived from a fungus that grows on rye or from morning glory seeds.

marijuana—A mood-altering drug made from the dried flower clusters of the hemp plant. Marijuana, widely known as either "grass" or "pot," is smoked in a kind of cigarette called a joint.

mescaline—The primary psychoactive ingredient found in peyote cactus buds.

methamphetamine—Often called crank, a form of amphetamine illegally manufactured for street sale as a stimulant.

morphine—The principal psychoactive ingredient in opium. It is generally used as a pain reliever or sedative.

narcotic—Originally a group of drugs producing effects similar to those of morphine. Today it often refers to any substance that sedates, depresses and/or can be addictive.

neuron—A nerve cell that passes signals to other nerve cells along a thread-like axon.

neurotransmitters—Electrochemical messengers that travel between brain cells and are responsible for all brain activity.

opiate—Any sedative or painkiller that includes opium, morphine, codeine, or heroin.

opium—A narcotic derived from the juice of the opium poppy, it is the source of all analgesics that affect the central nervous system.

overdose—A large quantity of a drug taken either accidentally or on purpose that causes temporary or permanent damage to the body and may be fatal.

paranoia—A tendency to suspect and mistrust others to the extreme.

peyote—A psychedelic cactus that grows in Northern Mexico and the southwestern United States.

phencyclidine—Also known as PCP or angel dust; generally mixed with other drugs to enhance their effects, it can produce terrifying hallucinations or psychotic reactions.

physical dependence—An adaptation of the body to the presence of a drug so that when the drug is not used withdrawal symptoms result.

psychedelic—A term used to describe the consciousness-expanding effects of such drugs as LSD, mescaline, and peyote.

psychoactive—Altering mood and/or behavior.

psychological dependence—A condition in which the drug user craves a drug to maintain a sense of well-being and feels discomfort when deprived of it.

psychosis—Basic mental dysfunction characterized by loss of contact with reality.

sedative—A drug that produces calmness, relaxation, and, at high doses, sleep.

sedative hypnotics—One of four primary psychoactive drug groups, used to control psychic pain and suppress activity.

synapse—The gap between the dendrites of one neuron and the dendrites of another.

synthesis—The laboratory process of creating a chemical compound by combining elements or simpler compounds.

tolerance—Decreased response to a drug after repeated use.

toxic—Poisonous.

tranquilizer—A drug that has calming, relaxing effect, such as Valium™.

withdrawal—The physiological and psychological effects of discontinued use of a drug.

Further Reading

Bennett, William. *The Index of Leading Cultural Indicators.* New York: Simon & Schuster, 1994.

Carroll, Marilyn. *PCP, The Dangerous Angel.* New York: Chelsea House Publishers, 1985.

Clayton, Lawrence. *Designer Drugs.* New York: Rosen Publishing, Inc., 1994.

Hafen, Brent Q. and Kathryn J. Frandsen. *PCP, Phencyclidine, "Angel Dust."* Center City, Minn: Hazelden Foundation, 1988.

Hales, Diane. *Case Histories.* New York: Chelsea House Publishers, 1987.

LaFountain, William L. *Setting Limits: Parents, Kids & Drugs.* Center City, Minn: Hazelden Foundation, 1982.

McCormick, Michele. *Designer Drug Abuse.* New York: Franklin Watts, 1989.

Robbins, Paul. *Designer Drugs.* Springfield, N.J.: Enslow Publishers, Inc., 1995.

Seymour, Richard, David Smith, Darryl lnaba, and Mim Landry. *The New Drugs: Look-Alikes, Drugs of Deception and Designer Drugs.* Center City, Minn.: Hazelden Foundation, 1989.

Internet Addresses

The World Wide Web has greatly enhanced access to reputable and authoritative information on PCP. Information is current, often available without a trip to a library, and relatively easy to find. Most government agencies and professional organizations now make many of their resources available electronically on the web. Previously these publications were typically available only in print and only by request or from a library.

On the other hand, with more than one billion indexable web sites to choose from, it is difficult to find exactly what you want. A search engine may retrieve thousands of sites. How do you find the ones you need? Even worse, there is a lot of inaccurate, confusing, and even strange information available on the web. Anyone can "publish" anything on the web! There are no requirements that the information be verified or reviewed before it is made available. Web sites may not be stable and can disappear at any time.

This chapter identifies and annotates some of the best, most authoritative, and stable sites on the web which deal with PCP.

Internet Addresses researched by: Greg Byerly and Carolyn S. Brodie are Associate Professors in the School of Library and Information Science, Kent State University and write a monthly Internet column titled COMPUTER CACHE for *School Library Media Activities Monthly.*

WEB SITES WITH INFORMATION ON PCP

As a Matter of Fact: Hallucinogens and PCP
<http://www.well.com/user/woa/fshallu.htm>
Produced by the Missouri Department of Mental Health, this site answers questions such as: "What is PCP?" and "What are the physical effects of PCP?" Also answers "Why is PCP dangerous?" and "How do PCP users feel?" Also covers LSD and mescaline and details their effects and dangers.

Adult Health Advisor: Phencyclidine Hydrochloride (PCP)
<http://www.brain.com/health_a2z/crs/pcp.htm>
Effectively warns against the use of PCP and suggests various lifestyle changes which can help individuals stay away from PCP and other illegal drugs. Describes not only the effects of PCP use, but also lists the symptoms of PCP abuse and how to treat it.

Clubdrugs.org
<http://clubdrugs.org/>
This site was cooperatively launched in December 1999 by the National Institute on Drug Abuse and four national organizations to "alert teens, young adults, parents, educators and others about the dangers of club drugs such as Ecstasy, GHB and Rohypnol, which are often used at all night "raves" or dance parties and have potentially life-threatening effects." A good site for up-to-date information about all types of designer drugs.

Drug Finder: PCP
<http://www.drugfreeamerica.org/druginfo/drugInfo.asp?drugID=30>
A good description of what PCP looks like and how it is used. This drug information sheet from the Drug-Free Resource Net site of the Partnership for a Drug-Free America stresses the problems associated with PCP use. Both the short-term and long-term effects of PCP use are briefly outlined.

Fact Sheet: PCP
<http://www.scprevents.com/web/infosite/druginfo/pcpfact.html>
This fact sheet from the South Carolina Department of Alcohol and Other Drug Abuse Services (DAODAS) provides some relatively detailed information about PCP by answering a series of questions.

Some of the questions not covered as directly at other sites include: "How is PCP ingested?" and "Why do people use PCP?" Also answers "Is PCP addictive?" and "What is the link between PCP and violent behavior?"

Facts About Drugs: PCP/Angel Dust
<http://www.brantleycenter.com/fad/pcp-angeldust.html>
Describes what PCP is, what it does, and what it feels like to use it. Special emphasis is on how the use of PCP can hurt you and when you should get help.

LSD
<http://www.usdoj.gov/dea/concern/abuse/chap5/lsd.htm>
A part of the Drugs of Abuse web site presented by the U.S. Department of Justice Drug Enforcement Administration (DEA), this site briefly describes LSD, its history, use, and effects. Click on Drugs of Abuse Hallucinogens Chapter to access additional information on other types of hallucinogens.

PCP
<http://www.teenchallenge.com/main/drugs/pcppage.htm>
This site by the Teen Challenge World Wide Network provides concise and clear answers to seven basic questions about PCP: "What is PCP?" and "What Does PCP Look Like?" Also answers "What are the Physical Signs of PCP Usage?" and "Where Does PCP Come From?"

PCP
<http://www.straightfacts.com/wwwpages/pcp.htm>
Investigate the origin and medical uses of PCP, learn its short and long-term effects, and consider issues of tolerance, dependence, and legal status. Notes that PCP is also known as angel dust, elephant, and hog.

PCP (Phencyclidine)
<http://www.nida.nih.gov/Infofax/pcp.html>
The National Institute on Drug Abuse (NIDA) provides web access to a series of "infofax" on various drugs. This Infofax briefly describes the health hazards of PCP use. The extent of current use is also provided by using figures from various national studies, including the National Household Survey on Drug Abuse (NHSDA) and the Monitoring the Future Study (MTF). Treatment possibilities are also mentioned.

PCP & Ketamine: A Selected Bibliography

<http://www.doitnow.org/pages/359.html>

This bibliography from October 2000 cites print articles and other materials on PCP and ketamine. Articles are from such journals as FDA Consumer, Journal of the American Medical Association, Nature.

Phencyclidine (PCP)

<http://www.usdoj.gov/dea/concern/pcp.htm>

This brief overview of PCP is presented by the U.S. Department of Justice's Drug Enforcement Administration (DEA). Adverse effects are enumerated and pictures of the drug as commonly sold are included.

Street Terms: Drugs and the Drug Trade

<http://www.whitehousedrugpolicy.gov/streetterms/>

Go to this site and then click on PCP. A list of over two-hundred names for PCP and terms associated with it use, especially in combination with other drugs, will be retrieved. Links are also provided to lists of terms associate with the Drug Trade, Drug Use, and Costs & Quantities.

GENERAL DRUG SITES WITH INFORMATION ON PCP

American Council for Drug Education

<http://www.acde.org/>

The American Council for Drug Education (ACDE) is "a substance abuse prevention and education agency that develops programs and materials based on the most current scientific research on drug use and its impact on society." The site offers extensive materials for youth, college students, parents, health professionals, educators, and employees. The following substances are covered by the site: Alcohol, Cocaine/Crack, Heroin, Inhalants, Marijuana, Methamphetamine, and Tobacco. ACDE is associated with Phoenix House, a nationally recognized leader in the treatment of substance abuse (http://www.phoenixhouse.org/).

D.A.R.E.

<http://DARE.com/>

This is the official site of D.A.R.E. (Drug Abuse Resistance Education). In addition to providing news about the D.A.R.E. organization, this site offers D.A.R.E. Kids, an interactive and fun site for kids with its own Clubhouse.

Get It Straight: The Facts About Drugs

<http://www.usdoj.gov/dea/pubs/straight/cover.htm>

This site includes the full-text of *Get it Straight! The Facts about Drugs*, published by the U.S. Department of Justice's Drug Enforcement Administration. It is designed to help teenagers "realize that using drugs is not the way to go. The book will also be helpful as a research tool for your school assignments, as something fun to read, and also as something to share with your friends." Each section deals with a specific category of drugs. Questionnaires, word searches, and other fun exercises are included in this hypothetical class assignment for teenagers.

Moyers on Addiction

<http://www.pbs.org/wnet/closetohome/home.html>

Companion to the five-part 1998 PBS television series, Moyers on Addiction: Close to Home. Host Bill Moyers looked at the science, treatment, prevention, and politics of drug addiction in the United States. This site continues to provide guides for each of the topics covered in the five episodes. In addition to providing background information and facts about addiction, in each case the experience of addiction is vividly described by someone who has experienced it. Animated graphics are used to demonstrate the effects of drugs on the brain and body.

Narcotics and Substance Abuse

<http://usinfo.state.gov/topical/global/drugs/>

Information from the U.S. Department of State concerning drug trafficking and substance abuse. Key documents in U.S. drug policy are available and links are provided to the principal federal agencies which deal with drugs in the United States. This is a good source for up-to-date statistics and other information about drug use, drugs and crime, and prevention and treatment.

Narcotics Anonymous

<http://www.wsoinc.com/>

Starting in 1947 as an outgrowth of Alcoholics Anonymous, Narcotics Anonymous, this site primarily deals with organizational news and history. However, it does provide access to numerous Public Information Guides and other information about narcotic addiction.

National Center on Addiction and Substance Abuse at Columbia University

<http://www.casacolumbia.org/>

Known as the Center for Addiction and Substance Abuse (CASA), this organization presents a wide variety of information on the impact and cost, both to individuals and communities, of drug use and abuse. Two sections of the site are especially useful. Resources and Links provides a wide-ranging lists of links to drug-related web sites in categories such as Federal Resources, Grant Making and Funding Resources, Kids and Teens Resources, Nonprofit Resources, Treatment and Recovery Resources, and Web Search Resources.

National Clearinghouse for Alcohol and Drug Information (NCADI) PREVLINE: Prevention Online

<http://www.health.org/>

PREVLINE, Prevention Online, is the web site for the National Clearinghouse for Alcohol and Drug Information (NCADI). NCADI is a service of the Center for Substance Abuse Prevention, which is under the Substance Abuse and Mental Health Services Administration (SAMHSA). The site includes Research Briefs, Workplace Issues, Resources & Referrals, Related Links, Alcohol & Drug Facts, Funding/Grants, Online Forums, and a Kids Area.

Girl Power!

<http://www.girlpower.gov/index.htm>

Girl Power! is a national public education campaign sponsored by the U.S. Department of the Health and Human Services to "help encourage and motivate 9- to 14- year-old girls to make the most of their lives." There are separate sections for girls and parents, as well as Research and News About Girls. While this fun site is about all aspects of girls' health, it includes information about the harmful effects of drugs on young women.

For Kids Only

<http://www.health.org/features/kidsarea/INDEX.htm>

This site NCADI is "For Kids Only." Visually appealing and lots of fun, games and other activities are used to address such issues as "Be Smart,

Don't Start" and "Internet Safety." Answers are also suggested for questions such as "How Can I Say No?" and "How Can I Help Someone?" Great for elementary and middle school students. This site is also available in Spanish.

National Institute on Drug Abuse

<http://www.nida.nih.gov/>

The National Institute on Drug Abuse (NIDA) is an agency within the U.S. Department of Health and Human Services. This site includes research findings, news releases, publications, legislation information, and links to other NIDA resources. Like NCADI, NIDA is an excellent source for accurate and informative materials about all aspects of drug use and abuse.

Commonly Abused Drugs: Street Names for Drugs of Abuse

<http://www.nida.nih.gov/DrugsofAbuse.html>

Similar to Information on Common Drugs of Abuse, this web page provides a chart which lists street names, medical uses, delivery systems, and other information for various Stimulants, Hallucinogens, Opioids and Morphine Derivatives, and Depressants.

Office of National Drug Control Policy

<http://www.whitehousedrugpolicy.gov/>

The Office of National Drug Control Policy (ONDCP) is a great source for information on a variety of drug-related topics. It sponsors and supports a wide variety of other web sites.

Drugs Facts and Stats

<http://www.whitehousedrugpolicy.gov/drugfact/drugfact.html>

A great source for statistics and facts about drug use and abuse in the United States. The Facts and Figures section provides direct access by drug name to an overview of the problem with the specific drug and current statistics on its prevalence.

National Youth Anti-Drug Media Campaign

<http://www.mediacampaign.org/mg/index.html>

The Media Gallery of the National Youth Anti-Drug Campaign provides direct access to current promotional efforts using television, print, radio, and banner ads.

FreeVibe

<http://www.freevibe.com/>

Freevibe was developed by the White House Office of National Drug Control Policy in collaboration with the Center for Substance Abuse Prevention (CSAP) and other partners. The site is visually appealing and designed to attract youths 11-14.

Partnership for a Drug Free America

<http://www.drugfreeamerica.org/>

The Drug-Free Resource Net of the Partnership for a Drug-Free America (PDFA) is an excellent source for fairly detailed information about many different drugs, including Marijuana, Inhalants, LSD, PCP, Peyote, Cocaine/Crack, Designer Drugs, Steroids, Tobacco, Alcohol, and Heroin. You can click on "What the drugs look like" to find pictures of drugs and you can go to "Paraphernalia" to find pictures of drug paraphernalia.

Planet Know

<http://www.planet-know.net/first.htm>

Planet Know, a Planet Free of Drugs, is a site designed to attract teenagers—it's animated, colorful, and creatively designed. Teens can dial "411" and take a quiz about Marijuana, Inhalants, Heroin, Hallucinogens, and Cocaine. This site needs to be explored to uncover all of its attractions.

Index

127